M000211336

THE POWER OF YES
Stacey Hall – Executive Producer
Lil Barcaski - Producer

GWN Publishing
GhostWritersNetwork.com
A Division of LongBar Creative Solutions, Inc. (LBCS)
LongBarCreatives.com

Edited by: Katelyn Stewart and Linda Hinkle

Book Layout & Cover Design ©2021 GFADDesign.com
Cyndi Long - LBCS/GFADDesign *GFADDesign.com*

ISBN: 978-1-7367932-0-6

IV • STACEY HALL

CONTENTS

Foreword

I've been personally involved in the network marketing profession now for nearly 20 years.

For the last 10+ years, my organization (My Lead System Pro) has served the network marketing industry by directly teaching and training independent distributors how to grow their business using the internet.

I have personally seen how the industry has positively impacted thousands of people I've known over the years.

What I have always loved about the network marketing industry is how it is the ideal vehicle to introduce entrepreneurship to people who've never before started a business yet have the drive and desire to take control of their financial security and their future.

It is a vehicle that breaks down the many barriers to entry that stand in the way of most people being able to start their own business.

For a relatively small financial investment (with such little risk and free of all the typical burdens of traditional business), any individual who has the desire and the drive can get started learning the critical skills required to grow their income as an entrepreneur.

It's little wonder that the network marketing industry continues to experience such tremendous growth, especially in times of economic instability.

We, at MLSP, are very encouraged that a book such as this has been published and sold through major booksellers.

We see it as one more way to inspire, empower, and educate millions of people around the world to explore and consider the network marketing industry as a viable and legitimate option to take control of their paycheck, their financial security, and their future.

Our way at MLSP, is to show entrepreneurs how easy it is to now be able to communicate with thousands of potential prospects all around the world using social media websites.

By learning a few simple skills and techniques, you can build your own global networks of people matching your ideal audience from the comfort of your home, even while working in your pajamas.

The internet has made the dream of a home-based business even more real than ever before.

Sadly, too many people give up on their dreams; too many people, settle for what they have, for what their boss offers them, what the government gives us and what the economy determines.

It is incredibly inspiring to see this book and imagine how many more people may be inspired to take that leap into entrepreneurship, to rediscover their passion and their dreams and to finally be able to make progress towards their financial goals.

The time is ideal for a book like this. Share it with those you love.

~ Norbert Orlewicz, Co-Founder, My Lead System Pro
book.goforyeschallenge.com

DEDICATION

This book is dedicated to those in the Network Marketing industry – the distributors, representatives, members, and consultants – who strive every day to make the world a better place by demonstrating the highest level of business ethics and person-to-person service to consumers.

ENDORSEMENTS

"Dreams do come true. Yes, even YOURS. But you have to meet them part way. Get this book as the first step towards them. Read it. Do it. Expect Miracles!"

- Dr Joe Vitale, author Zero Limits,
one of the stars of the hit movie, "The Secret."

"Network Marketing is the most powerful way for the average person to create financial independence and personal freedom."

~ Jim Packard, co-author of The Consistency Chain for
Network Marketing, www.consistencychain.com

"The Network Marketing industry is by no means new, but thanks to social media & attraction marketing, global opportunities and the level of professionalism, the network marketing business model is one the smartest options to build your financial future and create a legacy for your family.

Stacey Hall, the globally recognized author of books on Attraction Marketing, knows first-hand what it takes to build a successful network marketing business online and off. This time, she has brought together some of the leaders in our profession, each one with a story that will make you stop and think, "Is this for me? Should I explore my options further? What is my Plan B? "Don't ignore that intuitive voice. This book is all you need to join forces with a supportive community of entrepreneurs who are changing the world by helping others improve their lives."

~ Jackie Sharpe, Empowering Entrepreneurs and Network Marketers to Create the Life They Truly Deserve, www.EmpoweringEntrepreneursInstitute.com

"The network marketing industry has been such a blessing! It has allowed me more time and financial freedom than I ever imagined! Not only do I get to create my perfect day EVERY DAY, but I can do it from anywhere in the world! If you are looking to up your skills in network marketing, I am THRILLED for you that you have picked up this book! Do yourself a favor and read it from cover to cover and implement what you learn!"

~ Erin Birch, network marketer, business and personal transformation coach and trainer www.erinbirchcoaching.com

"This is a must-read guide for anyone considering Network Marketing, each author offers thought-provoking tips for creating your dream life."

~ Antonio Thompson, Marketing Agency Owner www.antoniorthompson.com

"Network marketing can be life changing! I've seen it first-hand and it has directly impacted my own business through our customers. This book can be a powerful tool to make network marketing life-changing for you, too!"

~ *Haylee Crowley, Owner Whimsy +Wellness*
www.whimsyandwellness.com

"This book is a "must-read" for all Network Marketers and aspiring Network Marketers. I am so grateful to see so many inspiring individuals who are playing BIG in life come together and create this incredible publication which will inspire and help thousands. It is definitely a book that I will reference over and over again."

~ *Elsa Morgan, Network Marketer,*
Coach, Speaker & Author
www.elsamorgan.com

"The ability to focus amidst the chaos of ongoing life is a vital and essential skill for successful living. Each of the Authors of "The Power of YES…" have created and share how they have prioritized what is most important to them. Their tips for navigating daily challenges can help you do the same and achieve the quality of life you envision and desire."

~ *Tara Rayburn, Healthy Habits Community*
Curator, www.healthyhabitscommunity.com

LIFE BY DESIGN

By Kim Ward

I remember December 28, 2014, like it was yesterday. How could I not? Some people go an entire lifetime without receiving the kind of call that I did that day.

At eight months pregnant, I looked at my husband and said, "Let's go!" We weren't traveling to the hospital; we drove to my mother's house because I recieved a phone call indicating that mom had killed herself.

Many thoughts and emotions were racing through my body. There was absolutely no way my mother would kill herself knowing what my family and I went through seven years prior when my 22-year-old sister Katie died by suicide. As I was about to give birth to my second daughter, I knew how much mom wanted to be a part of this exciting journey. We, as a family, had just celebrated our best and brightest Christmas, and there was so much joy around us.

When my husband and I arrived at "the scene," as it was referred to at the time, my mother's house was surrounded by lots of blue police lights. I franticly looked at my husband, who was a Lieutenant with Fire Rescue, and asked, "Where is the rescue?" Very calmly, he informed me that there was no need. My mother had indeed killed herself.

I was five months pregnant with my first daughter seven years prior, and I lost my only sister to suicide. At the time, I was working as a clinical laboratory manager, so I was at the mercy of my company's bereavement policy, which was only one week off for an immediate family member's death. One week was not enough time for me to wrap my head around everything that was happening, but I had responsibilities and had to work whether I liked it or not.

This time around, it was almost like a light switch flipped. I would NOT return to a job outside my home or miss any precious moments with the daughter that I would soon be giving birth to. Losing both my sister and my mother showed me that we never know how much time we truly have. Then and there, I decided not to work away from my family to earn money and then give that money to someone else for them to watch my child while I worked. That cycle was no longer working for me.

Thanks to Facebook, I connected with an amazing woman who introduced me to her product and business opportunity. She saw how tired I was from just giving birth and still processing the loss of my mother. She offered me a sample of her wellness products, and just like that, I became what those of us in network marketing call a "Day-oner"— individuals who see immediate results from our products.

"Ignorance on fire" is what I was commonly referred to after that. I saw the benefit of the product, and I was ready to run! Within seven months, I earned the monthly car bonus and purchased the BMW that I had always wanted to own. My team and I were recognized for hitting sales goals, bonus goals, and advancing in the ranks. I even earned two paid vacations. My "upline" and I worked together to help other members of our team hit their bonuses (and wellness goals) in record time.

About a year and a half into my network marketing journey, I began to self-sabotage. I was basing my worth on other people's results, and therefore, the lack of results was feeding into my limiting beliefs. That began an unhealthy cycle of "company hopping," which led to feeling like a failure. I even considered quitting network marketing altogether, but I knew the value of pushing through.

Thank goodness I was introduced to coaching and the importance of personal development. Through various mentorship programs and various self-development courses, I received the training and skills needed to relaunch my network marketing journey successfully.

As of now, this incredible industry has helped me fully retire my husband and give our daughter a life that we could have never given if we were still both working outside of the home. My dream was to raise my daughter and experience every moment of her life. She is now six years old and has been with my husband and me every single day. Network marketing has made our dreams come true—all from one simple word—Yes!

Contact the Author: Kim Ward
Email: Kim@lifebydesignsolutions.com
Visit: www.lifebydesignsolutions.com

Letting Pet Food Be My Medicine

By Amelia A. Johnson

Many years ago, I had a pet sitting and dog obedience business. I was constantly working—seven days a week and often 12-14 hours a day taking care of dogs, cats, birds, and even horses. Whatever animal was in front of me, even huge reptiles, I never really had time for myself, my husband, or my pets.

It was very frustrating to realize that no matter how hard I worked and how many employees I had my income was still going to be limited. I knew I would never be able to have the time freedom that I longed for to spend with friends and family; I would be on the hamster wheel forever, even though I loved what I did.

I did not know what else I could do since I preferred to have my own business and set my hours. I had already tried a dog-grooming business, and I also trained show horses, but these were also very time-consuming and limited-income careers.

Businesses are grown by fulfilling other people's needs and wants. Over time, I became very concerned about the health of the pets in my care. So many were aging too quickly. Their coats lacked luster and were easily mattered. Some pets were downright cranky. Others could barely make it up and down the stairs. I knew my clients wanted to have happier and healthier pets.

I have always believed in the expression "Let food be your medicine."

At that time, in 2002, there were few options when it came to pet food. A holistic vet encouraged me to get samples of better food from a pet food health store. My elderly dog chose one out of the 12 samples from smaller companies.

Then, out of the blue, I received a postcard in the mail offering a free sample of pet food by a new direct sales company. I sent for the sample, and my dog loved it more than any of the other choices he tasted. Despite his having Cushing's disease, my dog thrived on the food and treats I purchased from that company.

I saw that there was an opportunity to sell these products directly to my clients to also benefit their pets. However, because I had become so cynical about the pet food industry, I decided to meet the company's co-founders, the product formulator, owners, and staff before promoting the products to my clients. It was obvious to me that they loved pets and wanted to provide exceptional food, treats, and products for them, so I started telling my clients how their pets could also benefit from the company's products.

My clients also noticed how much healthier their pets were becoming, how vibrant they now were, and that they only had to go to the veterinarian for yearly checkups or acute issues rather than chronic disease. They thanked me and spread the word.

Once I understood the concept of network marketing and the possibilities for a larger income while working fewer hours, I welcomed others to join me as team members. My income check grew as their passion for helping pets expanded.

When I had to close my traditional business to care for my aging parents, instead of feeling panicked, I was grateful that I still had a sizeable income from the network marketing company. I was able to spend priceless time with my parents as they transitioned from this earthly life.

Now, I can spend more time with my husband, and I can show my dog wherever and whenever I want. I am happy that I can do my business from anywhere and at any time, even on my phone.

Naturally, because of all the animal-related businesses I have had, I absolutely love helping other people enjoy their lives with their pets. This company proves to me on a daily basis that it's here to stay. I am confident that my team will also be able to build a life with this company as they join me in helping people and their pets continue to thrive, be happy, and see possibilities that they never saw before for their own life.

My dream life began with the search for healthier pet food. God winked, and I received a direct mail invitation from a network marketing company that has helped me fulfill my desire not only for time and financial freedom but for healthier and happier pets.

Contact the Author: Amelia Johnson
Email: Amelia@ameliaAjohnson.com
Phone: 301-539-2393
Visit: www.ameliaajohnson.com/AMSgift

From Home Party Failure to Legacy-Building Success

By Barbara Levitt

It was in the late '60s when I made my first foray into network marketing. One of my husband's colleagues told us about a business opportunity—a skin care and cosmetics company. On a leave of absence from my teaching job to be a stay-at-home mom, this seemed like a way for me to contribute to our income. For a small investment, I received a makeup travel case filled with an assortment of products.

Following the home-party model endorsed then, and still endorsed today by many top- ranking professionals in the network marketing industry, I let my friends and family know what I was up to. I managed to book a few home parties and even got a few "pity purchases." Not nearly enough to cover the cost of my initial investment. My husband urged me to keep going, but I disliked what I was doing. I had run out of friends to ask to arrange parties. The makeup was certainly no better than the commercial brands I'd been using. I didn't love it. I decided to use the products myself until they ran out. That was a disaster! Never before did I have breakouts like I did with those products. In my gut, I knew there was no way I could sell something that I wouldn't use, that I didn't believe in, that could even be harmful. So as quickly as I was in business ... I was out! The most important takeaways from that experience were to use the products myself and to thoroughly vet a company before getting involved with it. I won't ever sell anything I don't believe in.

Fast forward to 2015 when my daughters surprised me, with an essential oils starter kit and a membership account for my birthday. My older daughter, Sharon, a licensed yoga therapist, uses essential oils personally and with her clients. Kim, an audiologist, uses essential oils for her family, and has a modest "oily" side hustle. Meanwhile, I was buying oils at health food stores and local markets, but not seeing (or feeling) any particular benefits. I didn't even like the way they smelled! Almost two months after getting the kit, I finally opened one bottle: lavender. Then I opened another bottle and then another. No more store-bought oils for me! I played with the oils in my kit. I searched for more information and learned so much about oils and about this company, and I must tell you—I'm still learning!

There are so many reasons why I love this company: outstanding product quality, product diversity to meet the needs of any age group from newborn to old age and regardless of gender, and we have products for animals/pets. The company is also generous in its compensation plan, supportive of its reps and has the best customer service!

Anyone desiring a toxin-free home and/or lifestyle needs these essential oils. We have high-quality plant-based personal hair and skin care products, makeup, nutritional supplements, home cleaning and CBD products. There are even some FDA-approved over-the-counter medications.

I use oils for energy, to support my immune system, help me focus and sleep better when I feel stressed. They do more than make my house smell good. Truthfully, there are too many uses to list here. When I fell and injured my wrist and shoulder, I could barely lift a coffee cup. A cream I made using a few drops of some of the oils offered some relief. My physical therapist said she loved it when I was her last appointment of the day because after she used my blend on me, her aching hands felt better.

Someone wanting a home-based business can take this as far as they want to go. There's nothing magical about it. Like any other business, you get as much as you put into it. Some of my friends (as does my daughter) have regular jobs, and they get a modest monthly check from this business that pays for their kids' music lessons, save for a vacation, or to hire a cleaning service.

They're growing their businesses while they're young so they can retire comfortably. I have a friend who lived in a low-income housing project for twelve years. She recently moved into a brand-new half-a-million-dollar home, has written several best-selling books on Amazon, and she has even developed her own programs as an outgrowth of her "little" oily network marketing business!

I've worked hard all my life. For many of those years, I was a single mom. My desire now is to leave a legacy for my children and grandchildren, to contribute to the well-being of those less fortunate, and to leave this world a little better than it is today. There are so many possibilities in this business, and life is so much easier if you go for "yes" with the right company, of course!

Contact the Author: Barbara Levitt
Email: wellnesswisdom4life@gmail.com
Website: www.BarbaraLevitt.com

FINDING INNER PEACE

By Carla Archer

"See, no one cares what you have to say," "Don't say anything at all," and "There is no value in what you are saying." Classic negative messaging like that used to play in my head.

Who cares what I had to say? Feelings of not being good enough used to be deep-seated beliefs I had lived with for a long time. All of this changed when I became involved with network marketing.

Known as quiet, shy, and an introvert to many, I knew this was not really who I was. I didn't know how to get the real me out! I struggled with insecurities that had (supposedly) protected me for so long, reactionary responses, feelings of guilt, sadness, shame, and self-bullying. I was not my authentic self.

Throughout my life, I have had many successes through work, relationships, financially, and personally. I had proven to myself that I could rise to the challenge, overcome, and succeed. Yet, I lived with insecurities that disguised themselves as protectors who kept me quiet and prevented me from experiencing inner peace, true happiness, and the creation of my dream life.

I discovered network marketing and my beloved company through a friend who had asked me to try the product. I had an amazing experience and right away thought, "Carla, there is something here for you."

Then my gut really started talking to me. Has that ever happened to you?

I knew deep down inside of me that there was something to this, something I needed to be a part of.

Did I know what that meant? Heck no! I knew nothing about network marketing. On top of that, I did not have any time (ever heard that one before?) to take on something new, oh yeah, and I was that super shy person, remember? Yet, all I could hear inside of me was, "Carla, YOU NEED to do this."

At the time, my world looked like this. My husband and I were busy getting another business up and running, and he needed my help and attention. We were "semi-retired," and we were working on creating time freedom in our life. I did not have my husband's help back then; (he is now my number one supporter) however, I was not sure if I should or how I would do this on my own.

What does a person do in this situation? Do you know the following quote by Sir Richard Branson? "If someone offers you a fantastic opportunity, but you are not sure you can do it, say yes — then learn how to do it later!"

It was such great advice, and I took it! Little did I know that I had just said YES to creating my dream life.

I am tearing up while I write this. You see, I have realized that I am now the best version of myself because of my network marketing business—I got her out!

Sometimes we think network marketing is all about money, time freedom, unique products, and working from home. You may not realize that to achieve all (or even just part) of this, you need to embark on a journey of self-discovery and personal growth.

My dream life has been created through network marketing by becoming the best version of me—YET.

The support, training, and opportunities to work through and overcome limiting self-beliefs are unending. Our industry realizes how we feel about ourselves, what we tell ourselves, and how we show up in our business is related to the results we get in our business.

I have often said that if you were to take away all my success in my four years in network marketing, the financial and time freedom, as well as the relationships, awards, and opportunities I have created, and leave me with who I am today, I would leave with a soul satisfied.

If asked to do it all over again, I would reinvest every minute of learning, discomfort, breakdowns, and breakthroughs to continue living as this version of me.

This has been my dream come true. The person I have kept inside for so many years can be free. I am living in alignment with who I know I am, and I can help others create their dream lives.

I have found my inner peace and have created my dream life, and I wish this for you too!

There is only one version of YOU; make it the BEST version possible.

Contact the Author: Carla Archer
Email: ecozonesocks@gmail.com
Visit: www.facebook.com/groups/
onlinebusinessguidewithcarlaarcher

FINDING MY TRUE PASSION

By Charlice Arnold

I've always enjoyed the idea of working when I want to and not because I have to and the concept of network marketing and residual income. I had unsuccessfully tried numerous direct sales companies over the years and settled on a freelance bookkeeping career.

After several years of working on my own for many small businesses, my marketing and accounting background led me to start a business with my boyfriend and another friend in the swimming pool products industry. While I enjoyed what I did—we created a successful business that allowed us to travel the world, make a lot of friends, live in a beautiful home and work from practically anywhere … plastic swimming pool fittings, drains, and jets just were not my passion.

Years later, when my husband passed away from cancer and sold my shares of the business, I finally had some time to figure out what I wanted to do, something that I could be passionate about. I knew that sitting at a desk all day crunching numbers for someone else's business was not something that would make me happy or successful in the long run. I wanted something more, something that I could call my own.

During this time of exploration and finding myself, I started working out more and paying more attention to my health. My goal was to avoid getting cancer or some other debilitating disease like my husband had suffered through. By this time, I had developed chronic back pain. It was so excruciating that some days that I could not work out or even sit down comfortably. I thought I would have to live with that pain forever.

That's when a good friend of mine said that she had some products that could help. I didn't know anything about them, but I had already spent so much on chiropractors, massage, acupuncture, and other holistic methods, I figured why not give them a try? I found mind-blowing pain relief almost immediately. A bonus with these products—I released some of the grief that I was still holding onto from my husband's death. My overall health started improving, and I had a ton of energy and a renewed outlook on life. My friend also began educating me about how many harmful products I was using every day in my home that were slowly poisoning my body.

I was blown away, and I wanted to share this knowledge with everyone I knew in hopes that they, too, could avoid getting deadly diseases like cancer. It was then that I made it my mission to become a wellness and toxin awareness educator. My network marketing business had all the products, tools, and community to make that happen. Of course, I had to get out of my comfort zone and still do all the work necessary to start making money with this business. This can be the most challenging part of network marketing, in my opinion. Sticking with it, finding strategies that work, and being consistent have been key for me. Feeling "salesy" or pushy was a struggle (for me) in the beginning. Then I realized that I was serving others and sharing something important and rewarding with them. Now, I find solace in knowing that, while this lifestyle and business may not be for everyone, it can be rewarding for those that "get it." There will always be people that are not receptive, or perhaps it's just not their time to hear what I have to say, and I'm okay with that. It took me a while to get to that place of not taking things personally or being attached to any outcome so that I could enjoy meeting people where they are at.

I find it satisfying to introduce my friends and family members to this lifestyle of fewer harmful toxins and amazing wellness products. Since I have been doing this business, I've met a fantastic community of men and women. I've been able to travel and educate everywhere I go, and my residual income increases every month. I enjoy attending and hosting wellness events, sharing on social media, and helping others reach their health and financial goals. I work because I want to, not because I must. Network marketing has enabled me to do what I love and am passionate about, so it does not feel like I am working. I truly believe that my dreams are coming true, and I can see even more lofty dreams on my horizon. All because I said "Yes" to network marketing.

Contact the Author: Charlice Arnold
Email: hello@charlicearnold.com
Visit: www.charlicearnold.com

SELLING SERENITY

By Tina Guimar

February 5, 2017 was a turning point in my life. It was the day that would change my life forever. When would I wake up from the nightmare I was living?

It all started on Easter, April 5, 2015, the day we lost everything in a house fire. That should have been the turning point in my life but believe it or not, it wasn't. Putting my feelings and emotions aside, I kept on going and pushing through because I had to be strong, right? In these two years, I became bitter, depressed, anxious, and angry.

My family and I experienced numerous life-changing events between April 2015 and February 2017 when I received the most devastating call from my father in the middle of the night. My brother was gone; he had taken his own life. How could this be happening? Hasn't my family been through enough in such a short time? What the hell was going on? There were so many unanswered questions.

At this moment, I knew it was time. It was time to stop trying to be so strong, and it was time to swallow my pride. It was time to ask for help. I knew that if I didn't make some serious changes in my life, things would never turn around. I couldn't continue living this kind of life.

Before these events, I was a hardworking mom of two, working 60+ hours per week and attending school part-time. I felt too exhausted and run down to take care of myself at the end of the day. I was broke, overworked, and stressed out every single day. I found myself taking on way too much to prove that I could move up the corporate ladder.

In my early 20's, I was introduced to network marketing. I saw the opportunity it could provide and realized this could be life-changing for my family's future. I dug in and started learning. What I didn't realize was how hard it would be to make sales and get sign-ups. For the next several years, I moved from company to company, thinking it was the company or the product that explained why I was not making any money. Some people would say I was young and naive. I would say I was ambitious and knew there was a better way of life.

In 2014, I finally found a network marketing company that I could hang my hat on and call home. It felt right. I loved how the products made me feel. I loved being able to share it with others and make a difference in their lives as well. It was the first time I made any money in network marketing. Life was starting to feel good, but one of the things I had to let go of (after the fire) was my side hustle so that I could survive the devastating loss and rebuild our house.

One of the commitments I made after my brother died was to get serious about being an entrepreneur. I dove back into network marketing. I obtained certifications in life and business coaching, NLP, and mindfulness. I even obtained my Rhode Island real estate license. I learned the proper way to market and how to brand myself. I have been using these strategies since 2018 and have been able to build a successful brand while working full-time with help from my mentors and coaches.

My journey allowed me to find serenity and share that with others. Mindfulness, meditation, and gratitude are what helped me get back on my feet. Forget this business of living a fast-paced life because it makes most people miserable. We need to slow down and be present in the moment or as much as possible. It's time to enjoy what little time we have on this earth.

Selling serenity is about being happy, peaceful, and calm in all areas of your life, and it is a lifestyle! It is where you can experience real joy and fulfillment. It is where you can live out your dreams and change the future for you and your family. It is where you can unleash your potential and live the life you are meant to live. It's about doing what you love. It's about leveraging people and systems so you can achieve true time and financial freedom. Your greatest adventures lie ahead. Are you ready? It's your time.

Contact the Author: Tina Guimar
Email: Tina@TinaGuimar.com
Visit:www.tinaguimar.com

A Better Financial Education Than College

By Darlene Williams

Before joining my financial learning community, my finances were "tore up from the floor up" and I was living payday to Monday, head over heels in debt, averaging three to five overdrafts every single month.

Reality started to set in when my mother died on Christmas night in 2001. My youngest sister made a statement that hit me like a ton of bricks. She wished that she had the money to have been able to give mom a better quality of healthcare.

That statement stung me so hard, and it haunted me for a long time. I thought about it day and night.

I felt like someone was continually jabbing me in my heart. I couldn't bear the thought of putting my children in a position where they would have to entertain those thoughts.

I felt so helpless and frustrated not knowing which way to turn, especially when my youngest child just turned a year old.

I found myself widowed on Labor Day of 1986 while still in my 20s, and if that wasn't enough, my father passed away the Sunday before Thanksgiving less than 90 days later. I began searching for a way to create some additional cash flow for my household.

Tim, a friend of the family, invited me to look at a business opportunity in 1997. Through that connection, I received a phone call from one of the company's co-founders on October 23, 2005, saying, "Get ready. Get ready. Get ready!" I enrolled in the company that night and have been blessed ever since.

Since joining my financial learning community, those distasteful overdrafts no longer exist. I've opened and funded a brokerage account in addition to earning a thousand-percent return on my business. A business is truly your best investment.

Although my degree was in finance, I got my financial education from my network marketing company. Network marketing has leveled the playing field and allows anyone the opportunity for unlimited income potential. It's not how much you make that counts but how much you keep. You must learn how to make money work for you, or you will always work for money.

Education is the key to success. Why not learn and earn at the same time? Timing plus action will equal success. Financial freedom equals time freedom. If you don't fund your dreams, you'll always be working to fund someone else's.

Moms Mabley said it best—if you always do what you've always done, you'll always get what you've always got.

On the 40-40-40 plan, you work 40 hours a week for 40 years and take 40 percent of your working income in retirement. We're already tired; that's why they call it retirement because we go back to work and do it all over again.

Our government and corporate America tried to fix this situation with Social Security and pensions but couldn't.

My mentor, Alvin, told me that our company was built for the masses to win, realizing that everyone can't sell, and everyone can't recruit. But the masses can increase their cash flow by minimizing their taxes, eliminating their debt, and building great credit to attain personal financial success.

There's nothing wrong with a job. You need a job and a business to keep more of your money and strategize your way to wealth.

I'm super excited about helping Baby Boomers retire and build their own "stimulus" that keeps on giving. Before I retired from the Corrections industry, I realized that I wouldn't have enough money to stop working without building my business. I was a single mom with five children, two of which were heading to college. My pension alone wouldn't be enough. So, I applied the strategies in my home-based business's income-shifting membership to minimize my taxes, eliminate debt, and improve my credit score by over 100 percent.

Along the way, I got an investment education and became an owner and not just a loaner. It feels GREAT to own part of America!

Network marketing has afforded me the opportunity to generate unlimited income potential, given me time, freedom, and the finances to travel back and forth between two states to visit my grandchildren any time I want.

I'm so grateful that I can live the lifestyle I choose and provide for my family. As a financial literacy coach, I educate Baby Boomers on how they can grow their finances so that they won't be stressed. Most Baby Boomers fear they won't be able to retire or will outlive their income in retirement. I have proven financial strategies that can increase your cash flow to retire with financial security and peace of mind. It's my goal to help 10,000 Baby Boomers attain personal financial success. Wish me all the best!

Contact the Author: Darlene Williams
Email: darlene@darlenewilliams.com

Necessary Changes While the Work World Reboots

By Deb Willder

I have worked as an administrative assistant in various industries my entire adult life. There was nothing wrong with those positions other than they left me wanting more. I wanted time and financial freedom and being an "admin" wasn't going to get me there. I was surrounded by bad bosses, good bosses, and those in-between. Being an employee is not my bag, and I know many people feel the same.

Many might like their job but don't feel secure after 2020 "rocked" so many businesses. Many lost jobs, and many of those jobs may never come back. Work-life as employees will most likely never be the same.

When we were young, we were told to work hard, go to university, get a good job, and then work until retirement. That advice may have worked for some, but I often wondered if others secretly yearned for more.

Working as an employee was just not how I wanted to live. I didn't like having my lunch hours dictated to me. I couldn't just pop out of work when I felt like it. I couldn't always take a day off at a moment's notice. And, of course, there were many other restrictions.

It just was not the life I wanted for myself.

I joined a couple of network marketing companies, and they both had great products; however, in my opinion, the income I could make with them was limited. For example, earning $20 on a product meant that (to achieve my goal) I had to sell 500 each month. That involved some serious hustle.

I was introduced to my current company by a friend I met a few years before at a blogging workshop. She told me about this company that had the most incredible business education program with an option to partner with a high-ticket offer to earn maximum commissions. This company provided me with a rock-solid investment that was good for my health and the environment—winner!

I viewed a webinar on how it worked and was immediately sold. I had to get in! I could see my dream vision of cat motel/ sanctuaries being attainable with much less hustle and a lot less risk of burnout.

Continuing with low-ticket items was not likely to provide me enough income to quit my job in the foreseeable future; I now see it possible by the end of 2021. Not only that, but I am investing in my health as it is a product that is great for the environment and promotes low-toxic living and sustainability.

Network marketing came into my life via yet another friend who asked me if I wanted to achieve a particular result—to lose weight—that was an issue for me, and it was also a benefit of the product. However, I saw a few marketing tactics that were not in line with attraction marketing as I now know it.

My current company is all about attraction marketing; the concept of "know, like, and trust." The education they supply their marketers is "next-level!" Our platform's courses include a 30-day fast-start program for beginners and training on sales, marketing, money mastery, Facebook ads, the proper mindset, and everything our high-ticket item offers. On top of that, we get valuable masterclasses (included in our membership fee) from experts in their respective fields.

Our leaders come from varied backgrounds, and our Aussie founders were once broke and struggling to pay their rent and groceries. They punted, flew across the world to learn the business, and in 90 days, they were smashing it.

It can happen fast, or it can take a little longer; it will happen when it is meant to. We have the most incredible community that builds each other up, celebrates each other's successes, and helps each other when we need it. At the same time, we make sure each person becomes self-reliant.

I have yet to achieve the levels that my mentors have, but I plan to get there. I have my flag planted, and my vision for 2021 is to hand in my resignation letter for my current job so I can start 2022 as a self-employed "freedompreneur."

I have lofty yet attainable goals. I know I can achieve them because I have full confidence in myself and my business. I have achieved so much with self-confidence, the proper mindset, and personal growth—all of which are invaluable.

If any of this makes you want more, click on the links provided, and I will be in touch. Know that you can do it; the first step involves saying "yes."

Contact the Author: Deb Willder
Email: debwillder@gmail.com
Visit: www.debdwillder.com

A Traditional Business Owner's Journey into Network Marketing

By: Dena Soliman

In 2006, after finishing my last round of chemotherapy, I could officially count myself as a survivor of Hodgkin Lymphoma. It was at that time my husband asked me what I wanted to do next. I knew exactly what I wanted to do – own my own business. With an MBA and years in corporate America under my belt, it was time for me to achieve my ultimate goal of becoming an entrepreneur. Within just a few years, I was an on-site owner of a preschool with a staff of 45 employees. Despite how I learned in college and business school, it pales in comparison to the education I received, and continue to receive, as a business owner. Over the years, one significant aspect I've discovered is that the principles of traditional business and marketing are universal and can be applied to any industry. And it's around this that I've built my network marketing business.

As a traditional business owner, I spent years opposed to the idea of network marketing. I've purchased products from employees in order to help them out, but that's as far as it went. In 2016, however, that changed. After struggling with bald spots left by chemotherapy for a decade, I sought out a niche hairstylist for help. She sent me home with a product and in just two weeks, I began seeing results. Unbeknownst to me, it happened to be a network marketing product, but after seeing my hair redrawing and receiving compliments, I decided it was worth selling.

As I began my network marketing journey, I made the decision to do things my way. I knew it was possible to apply the strategies and principles I utilized in my brick-and-mortar business to selling a network marketing product. I just needed to adapt my real-world strategy for the online world. I knew I had a compelling story and a strong connection to the product – all I needed to do was get my voice out there and the product would sell.

Unlike many network marketers, I've only ever used Facebook. I believe it's important to keep it simple. By posting videos of me using the product, I began to gain a following and bring in sales. In under two years with the company, I made top rank and earned myself a director position.

With this proof of my strategy's success, I continued running my network marketing organization my way, grounded in the skills I'd learned as a traditional business owner. As my business grew and the number of people on my team increased, I saw a need for stronger, more hands-on leadership. A good leader can make or break someone's experience. Leadership is the difference between somebody turning $200 into $1000 of recurring monthly income or making nearly nothing and giving up. I wanted to not only be a strong leader, but to create them, as well.

Two years after starting my network marketing business, I began teaching classes. It became my mission to create entrepreneurs by teaching them the marketing strategies and principles used in the real world. At first, I taught five- and seven-day classes. However, as of last year, I've begun teaching 30-day courses. In them, I try to get it through to each student that their story is valuable. Getting out of your comfort zone and telling your story are fundamental aspects of a successful network marketing business. I teach them to show up and to be consistent. In my traditional business, I am an on-site owner – which is rare – but that is me, showing up. Each and every day, I'm there – giving tours, speaking to parents, bringing in new families. I teach my students that this level of being consistently present is as important to an online business as it is to a brick-and-mortar storefront. I provide my students with an arsenal of tools they can implement, and I hold their hand through each step – from their first Facebook post to their first sale. It's important to me that they understand the basics of business and are guided through the process in a way that sets them up for success.

I've watched network marketing change lives. And even though I still own and operate my preschool, this is my passion. I am compelled to help others – either through my products or my knowledge. And it's important to me that anyone I work possesses the same motivation. From my position, network marketing is servant leadership at its best. And as someone with over 12 years of experience as a traditional business owner, it is both my obligation and privilege to use my knowledge and skills to help others transform their lives.

Contact the Author: Dena Soliman
Email: dena.soliman@gmail.com
Visit: www.denasoliman.com

No More Trading Time for Money for Me

By Elaine Payne

Why would a critical care nurse, a nurse educator with three nursing degrees, choose network marketing after retirement?

Network marketing was not an avenue that I pursued to continue my happy dream life. I had already experienced what I felt was my dream life in nursing. This career had taken me through three nursing degrees, Adult and Pediatric Critical Care certifications, and on and on. Nursing was physically, emotionally, spiritually, and psychologically challenging every day that I worked, but I loved it—including the incredible, smart people I worked with. I loved making the worst days imaginable for patients and families the best that those horrible days could be. I appreciated and laughed out loud at the coping mechanism of humor in the healthcare industry. I enjoyed the challenge of all there was to learn and know. I enjoyed being part of miracles—where a person had a 1% chance of survival and the team that made them live. I cherished the continuing relationships, often with people whose loved ones had not survived.

Working in healthcare for so many years meant some "skewing" of life experiences. I worked holidays. I worked weekends. I missed many family gatherings. I even missed my surprise birthday party. I exchanged time and worked for money.

I found myself assessing everyone I saw from a health perspective. "That person's color was terrible. He really should be in the hospital." Most of these assessments occurred in elevators, where you have a moment to observe how people are breathing, looking, and acting. One morning, I was leaving work and in the elevator was a young man who looked to be in his early 20's. He was in a wheelchair being wheeled by an apparent friend of his, also in his 20's. The man in the wheelchair smiled and spoke as if nothing was wrong, but his color was gray, and his breathing too labored. They were heading to the Radiology Department for an x-ray. I said to myself; he will be a patient in the ICU tonight. And he was.

My salvation was, in fact, my salvation. My beliefs included that this life, as wonderful as it could be, was a brief layover for the destination of heaven with no pain, no hurting, no heartbreak, and no death. That belief system kept me in my career for over 40 years.

I retired. I celebrated that I would not work again. I was going to "play," design gardens, knit, travel, "go to lunch," and read novels. And I did! Four years later, I felt a gap—something was missing. That is when a friend said to me, "Come on. Do this with me. These products are great. It'll be fun." We had known each other for a long time. She was excited, she was smart, and I trusted her. I said "yes!" And that was how my experience in network marketing began. I did not know about network marketing at all.

I did not understand the beauty of network marketing, a mechanism that could make dreams come true. One specific and huge tidbit that opened my eyes was Robert Kiyosaki's grid that shows where 95% of income is based on trading time for money. I did not want any more of my time to be traded for money. I wanted residual income. I had been blessed, very blessed, with my previous income and an unexpected gift. But we had two children with families. They were my why. I wanted residual income and financial freedom for them. That residual income came from network marketing.

This past year, I consciously learned more about network marketing as I discovered the opportunities presented with network marketing. What other business could I do with minimal investment? What business provided me with exceptional products for wholesale prices? What business could I offer to those who needed financial (and product) assistance? What other business could make my dream of providing a legacy to our children come true?

My network marketing company was a "business opportunity." But that was not all it was. It taught me smart strategies through education and provided support where I met fun, positive, and intelligent people. This company offered me the chance to earn an income in four different ways and included financial guidance and investments in me. My company grew 700% last year with projections of quadrupling this next year. I worked from home, and I met new people from all over the world and built relationships with them. I could help others earn money and create their dream life. I could begin to see my future dream unfold. Why would anyone not say "yes" to this opportunity?

Contact the Author: Elaine Payne
Email: Peep1226@gmail.com

BETTER LATE THAN NEVER

By Elisa Mardegan

I was always that person who lived in the moment and never really thought much about the future. Don't get me wrong, I had dreams, but they were the typical "get a good job, marry a nice man, and have a family" kind of dreams. They weren't bad dreams, just not unique. I did not realize that I could still have a family and fulfill my purpose here on this earth by helping other women fulfill theirs.

It took a while, but I now have all three dreams, and it's so much better than I could have ever imagined!

Let me take you back a few years, about 23 to be precise. I moved back home after going to college for graphic design. A year later, I landed a decent-paying job with a great company. There wasn't anywhere to move up in the company, but I was happy, and the people I worked with were like my second family. Five years later, they ended up closing the business. I was fortunate, though, as I found another job in the advertising industry with more fantastic people.

One month after starting that job, a bomb landed in my life. I was diagnosed with breast cancer at the age of thirty-three. So, here I was in my thirties, with no husband (although an amazing boyfriend), no children, living with my mother, and now my life was put on hold.

I won't go into the nitty-gritty of that time period in my life, as that is a story for another time. However, I will say that everything eventually worked out, and my then-boyfriend has now been my husband for almost 17 years, and we have two beautiful children.

That part of my dream has come to fruition, although much later than I had initially anticipated.

I was incredibly blessed to stay at home with my children (another dream), but my days and nights were consumed with them, and I did nothing for myself. Fast forward a couple of years when I came across a website called Etsy. Of course, I just had to try it, so I opened a shop where I hand-stamped vintage silverware with cute sayings. It ended up being quite successful; however, I was not successful enough to hire help, so I was doing everything myself. We now had extra money, but I had no time freedom. Not exactly how I envisioned it, but I didn't want to give it up. Not just yet anyway.

After a couple of years of doing this, I came across someone who was sharing essential oils. At the time, I had no idea it was a network marketing company, let alone what network marketing even was. I was just interested in the oils and all the other clean products they offered.

After a few months of following her and seeing what it was all about, I finally decided to take the plunge! It was the best thing I could have done for myself. Not only was I using products that were chemical-free and better for my health, but I was also in a community of some of the most fantastic and encouraging people I have ever met. When I decided to try the business side of things, they answered all my questions and helped me get my business off the ground.

My dream didn't stop there. Being in network marketing has led me to even more incredible things. I am now coaching other women network marketers on creating a business based on building relationships instead of chasing people away by being a pushy salesperson. I have created a 6-step formula to success inside my Effortless Success Academy Coaching Program, and the ladies in this program are crushing it! I couldn't be prouder if I were their mother!

My dream now is to help female network marketers create a successful and effortless network marketing business by teaching them the skills required to build authentic relationships on social media and become extraordinary leaders for their teams.

It may have taken me longer to realize my purpose and how to find the perfect way of sharing it, but there is a saying, "Better late than never!"

Contact the Author: Elisa Mardegan
Phone: 519-903-6071
Email: elisa@elisamardegan.com
Visit: www.effortlesssuccesswithelisa.com
www.www.facebook.com/groups/
NetworkMarketingStrategiesforWomen

A LIFE WITHOUT LIMITATIONS

By: Erin Capezzera

For as long as I can remember, all I wanted was to become a nurse. Even as a kid I was goal-oriented – and being a nurse was that goal. Not only did it align with my desire to help others, but I also assumed it would be the perfect job for a mom.

It wasn't until I fulfilled my dream and entered the nursing field that I discovered this assumption couldn't be further from reality. At first, when I worked in hospitals, the salary was great, but the schedule was grueling. I then moved to teaching nursing in college; however, once I left teaching and began searching for jobs within private practices, I realized nurses don't make as much money as you might think. In fact, based on the job offers I received, my salary would have been pretty much equal to what I'd pay a high school student to babysit my kids while I was at work.

Once I understood the realities of nursing, I decided to be a stay-at-home mom. However, once my family went from having two incomes to just one, I realized we needed a little extra money. On top of that, I looked up and discovered I'd lost myself in motherhood. Don't get me wrong, being a mom is great – I love it to pieces and wouldn't trade it for the world – but I still craved goals, success and mental stimulation. And I missed that feeling of belonging to something bigger than myself that nursing provided me.

Then along came network marketing which seemed to check all the boxes. I could work around my kids' naptime, I wouldn't need a babysitter and if my husband were to get transferred, I could pick up my business and take it with me. Not to mention, starting my own business would definitely provide me with plenty of mental stimulation and goals. So, I decided to give it a try and see how it went.

Of course, it went horribly at first. I thought I knew what I was doing but soon realized I didn't have a clue. That is when I found an amazing coach who helped me find me again. I stopped chasing after the latest fad, started being my true and authentic self and chose the type of networking business that spoke to my heart. And things started to fall into place. The difficulty I had at the beginning forced me to make changes within myself and recognize who I truly am and what really matters to me.

That is when I found an amazing coach Kim Ward who helped me find me again and I stopped chasing after the latest fad.

I am driven to succeed. I am driven by a sense of community. And I'm driven by a deep desire to help others. Thanks to networking marketing, I'm achieving each of these.

While motherhood does involve goals, they are more long-term. It's hard to see results on a daily or weekly basis. However, with my network marketing business, I now am in a position to set and achieve goals with more frequency. I've had the opportunity to meet amazing human beings that I didn't even realize existed before.

Together, we share in our struggles and celebrate each other's victories. There's a real sense of camaraderie. And lastly, I get to help others. In fact, network marketing is set up in such a way that the more value you provide to others, the more money you make.

My network marketing business has allowed me not only to be a stay-at-home mom, but, for the last three years, a homeschool mom, as well. And once I stopped caring what others thought, disposed of my limiting beliefs and began living and working as my authentic self, I reaped many more rewards than just freedom and flexibility. I have conversations every day, like you would with your girlfriends, and then I hear later that I've impacted someone's life in a positive way.

I'm making money and simultaneously having so much fun. I'm pushed every day to be the best version of myself which not only makes me a better businesswoman, but also a better wife and mother. In order to succeed in this industry and truly help others, you must first grow and develop.

You have to be yourself and be vulnerable. Once you achieve that, you will be in a position to increase your income, stimulate your mind and enrich your soul.

Contact the Author: Erin Capezzera
Email:erin@decreaseclutter.com
Visit: www.decreaseclutter.com

It Wasn't Easy, But I'm All in Now

By Francine Mondi

Recently, an acquaintance of mine posted an article she had written about the dangers of network marketing. This struck a nerve with me, and I looked back at the events of my life over the last seven months because I used to be one of those people.

In July 2020, when we were five months into a two-week quarantine, I was feeling unsatisfied. I am a single mom and was working from home 90% of the time. My kids were at camp, and I was alone all day.

One day, I responded to a post on Instagram by an Emmy-winning actor/fitness expert about moms working from home. I never thought I would get a response, but I did. He was looking for women to join his team. Everything we talked about was what I was looking for. He offered me an opportunity to become a humanitarian entrepreneur, partner with a company that helps people, and then give back to their community to boot. It took a few conversations before I signed on, not because of lack of interest but because I had heard several negatives about network marketing. I asked a million questions, and he answered everyone with patience and kindness. Eventually, I decided to give it a try.

I wish I could tell you it was easy. I wish I could tell you I made thousands of dollars immediately. I wish I could tell you I lived happily ever after, but I didn't.

It was hard, very hard. I questioned whether I had made the right decision. However, the community of people I met when I joined this company was some of the most incredibly kind humans on this planet. I finally felt a sense of purpose, and it didn't matter that I wasn't financially successful yet. I was successful in my soul.

Fast forward to November. I decided I could no longer afford to "waste time" on my business and couldn't afford the products. My son needed expensive dental surgery and my anxiety and depression over the impending holidays became too much to handle. I convinced myself that no one would miss me and that everything I had felt when I was starting was a lie.

Within a day of me "closing shop," I got messages from several team members, including my coach, who I was sure didn't care about me because I wasn't making him money. They said they would be there to support my choice and that they loved me. But that's just the platitudes people say. No one means that, right?

A few weeks went by, and I was feeling even more depressed. How could I miss these people I had only known for a few months? They continued to reach out. I continued to fight the urge that I truly mattered to them. I convinced myself that they were just being nice and would move on quickly. Those thoughts paralyzed me with sadness. I was on the verge of darkness.

Author Roy T. Bennett said, "Do not let the memories of your past limit the potential of your future. There are no limits to what you can achieve on your journey through life, except in your mind." I let my past experiences and preconceived notions of network marketing influence my current actions and act as proof that I was making the right choice to walk away.

In December, I started to dip my toe back in because my company offered a significant cash incentive for the holidays, and it gave me an excuse to stay relevant to people that I missed. I needed that money, but truth be told, my heart wasn't in it. I felt like an imposter.

Two days after Christmas, I received a voicemail from my coach. He was apologizing for not responding to something I asked him ten days prior about the business. I didn't call him back because I just couldn't. I could barely speak about what I was going through without crying.

The next day, I spoke to a member of my team via text. I was honest with her about my situation and my feelings. I don't know why I finally spoke up, but I did. Something in my heart knew she was a safe haven to talk to.

Shortly after that, I got a message from my coach once more requesting I answer the phone the next time he called. I knew I couldn't avoid it forever, and I had already spilled my guts to one person, so I answered. He asked me how I was doing. I said, "I'm okay." He responded with, "You're not a good liar. I know you're not okay. What's going on?" It was like the flood gates opened. We had an incredibly honest talk. He knew so much of what was going on without saying a word. He reassured me that he was there for me and would do whatever he could to help me through my dark time. When we hung up, I felt like a huge weight had been lifted.

I found a way to start retaking the products. They are mental optimization products that kept my brain from betraying me. If I had never gone off them, I might not have had this epiphany—when you're in a bad place, you honestly believe what your mind is telling you. They are your thoughts, and they can't lie. Or can they? Trust me when I say they can, and they do. My perception of the situation was clouded, and it was nowhere close to reality.

So, long story short, while network marketing may not be the solution to my financial concerns yet, without this company, without these products, without these people, who knows where I would be? For me, that makes the reward so much greater than the risk.

I have become a certified mindset coach. I am on a journey of personal growth that will turn my dreams into goals and, ultimately, my reality. For that, I am forever grateful. I am all in.

Contact the Author: Francine Mondi
Email: francinemondi@gmail.com
Phone: 732-673-3168
Visit: www.linktr.ee/FiercelyFrancine

THE "AMERICAN" DREAM HELD AROUND THE WORLD

By Gail Woolsey

In Northern Ireland, when you mention network marketing, it brings up a variety of responses, such as: "That sounds like I'll have to pay loads to sell things for other people," or "That's just one of those American money-making schemes!"

Network marketing is a relatively new business concept in the United Kingdom (U.K.), and apart from the Amway parties my parents dragged us to back in the '80s, I didn't know much about it.

It's also true that network marketing is sometimes viewed as a "Get-rich-quick" scheme. People will frequently display their new cars, trips to Fiji, or great compensation plans as an incentive for others to jump on board. Although those fortunate few may have found their magic formula to overnight success, I've discovered it's not that simple.

Three years ago, I fell into doing business with my company. I have never considered myself a salesperson; in fact, I cringe at the idea! As a nurse of twenty years, caring for people was always my driving force when thinking about a career choice.

I'm very much a "blue personality," and much to my surprise and delight, network marketing requires self-reflection, personal growth, and pushing past my comfort zone to discover my strengths and the areas in my life that need work.

In hindsight, I'm glad I built my team at a slow pace. I had, and still have, a lot to learn about this business, and as an introvert and recovering perfectionist, I'm a continual work in progress!

I think this is why so many people talk about how network marketing changed their lives. It's not just some dramatic "catchphrase." The opportunity can honestly be transformational in your life, and it's not just the income opportunity that can be life-changing. Personal development comes first; the financial reward follows.

My "upline" is based in the U.S., so the market is a little different there than in the U.K., and although there are a wealth of resources and training available for new people to utilize, most people must find their way of doing the business side of things.

The good news is there are lots of ways to be successful in this business. Some people have been successful in doing in-person classes or blogging. Some are social media influencers and have hundreds of beautiful posts and pictures.

Merely suggesting a solution for specific issues friends and family happened to mention came naturally to me. And using the roller bottle of one of my stress-relieving products at work had people interested.

Everyone has a different way of making money, and no one way is right or wrong.

There's no one-size-fits-all approach to how you do network marketing. The most successful business builders use a combination of ways that work for their personality. That's how personal development comes into play!

I never had any intention of doing this business; I just needed the products!

After enduring a few health struggles with little support or options offered by my general practitioner, I happened to come across a video by a female physician with the sweetest Southern drawl. I immediately identified with a lot of the struggles she had, and I was all ears when she suggested I might try some essential oils and other products. I signed up with an essential oils starter kit which I immediately fell in love with and dove into all the training and information our team was so happy to talk about.

I joined various Facebook groups and loved the community aspect of the industry. I have met like-minded people from all over the world who crave a more holistic approach to wellness using high-quality essential oils.

The convention I attended in Brussels last year was one of the most memorable experiences I have ever had. Our company has a 25-year-strong foundation to stand upon, and I got to meet some of the scientific team and doctors behind the research and development that goes into our products. Many of the people I had met online and were meeting now (face to face) for the first time. It was a blast!

Our company's ethos of "people before profit" was vital for me. When I stumbled across the Compensation Plan, I almost fell off my seat as I realized I could also make a substantial income doing what I was already doing—talking about and sharing the fantastic oils that had worked so well for me.

As a nurse and a single mum, I had just about scraped by for most of my adult life. As I mentioned earlier, I have worked for the Health Service for over 20 years, and I have absolutely nothing to show for all those years of arduous work.

As a senior staff nurse, I also realized that unless I went into management (which I hated), I would never really be able to earn more than what I was now without putting in more long hours of blood, sweat, and tears. Honestly, I was exhausted. The pandemic pushed many of us over the limit of what we could bear.

In this business, I get to choose how much time and effort I put in. It requires some discipline, but the great part is that you can work around your schedule if you have another job or are a stay-at-home mum. As you gain confidence and build your team, the growth you make as a person is priceless and where the basis of your success will be.

If I do the work, the opportunity is golden. It's the so-called "American" dream, and thanks to the internet, it is also my dream. I just need to go for it and not give up.

Contact the Author: Gail Woolsey
Visit: www.gailforce100.goforyesnow.com

Building a Sisterhood Lifeline

By Geli Heimann

"Why did you not have it checked out earlier?" she demanded with a worried but indignant voice, with her hands on her hips and looking down at her mother in her hospital bed.

I was amused, but really, I had expected my daughter to give me a lecture as she unpacked all the various healthy goodies she had grabbed en route, rushing from work to see me. I ensured her I was okay as the nurse passed by with another syringe full of morphine for me.

I had been in pain due to my legs for months with what turned out to be severe acute cellulitis caused by bacteria in the deep layers of skin. The skin around the lower part of my legs had virtually come off. Medical staff and doctors were on high alert for life-threatening sepsis.

To be truthful, I did not have time to be sick. Plus, I felt like a failure.

Here I was with two science degrees, including a master's in business psychology. I had chosen to be a coach and consultant in private practice. Despite showing positive results with clients, I had no clue how to get new clients once they left.

With all my enthusiasm and love for my work, reality became rather self-evident—word-of-mouth is not predictable nor consistent in getting new clients.

I worked hard to make ends meet, chasing both clients and business leads alike but found myself still strapped for cash.

I was stuck in the typical self-employed/solopreneur conundrum— if I wanted to earn more, I needed to work more. The old "trading time for money" paradigm wasn't sustainable and did not work for me. With no leverage or systems in place, everything relied on me. I could not take a few days off when I needed to. I did not have a business. I had a j-o-b.

I looked good on paper with all my credentials. I was a business professional, an entrepreneur, and an exhausted hamster in a wheel, worried about paying my bills.

I worried about my financial future, especially as I was now over 60 years old, single again, and had no pension to enjoy. I realized I had become a professional academic statistic, particularly being a woman of that age group.

Then, my biggest fear became a reality—I needed a job, so I didn't have to live in a cardboard box under a bridge!

That is how I became a caregiver, receiving minimum pay while working with young people who had mental health challenges and those with severe learning disabilities such as autism, cerebral palsy, and other disabilities, including those who were wheelchair-bound. Now, I worked 70 daytime hours, interspersed with four nightshifts per week, while at the same time juggling client time and attempting to work my network marketing business.

Then, the inevitable happened—burnout, adrenal fatigue, fibromyalgia, damaged spine, and finally, my long stint in the hospital with cellulitis.

Here I was lying in a hospital bed, going nowhere fast with bandaged legs, cannulas for drips, and high-dose antibiotics via IV hanging from both arms and needing morphine for pain management.

At 65 years old with no pension to speak of, and clearly, without being able to return to the caregiver job, my future did not look rosy at all.

All I could do was pray. Renewed Hope in my Next Chapter

I was yearning for a different life. I knew that network marketing provided the potential for success, but I did not know how yet.

I had already joined a network marketing company, a health and well-being lifestyle company that produced therapeutic grade essential oils. Initially, it was not to build a business with but as a complementary tool to support my clients' emotional well-being during our sessions.

I decided to make network marketing a viable part of my multi-stream of income proposition. After all, the essential oils were a perfect and complementary match in a health and wellness mindset coaching practice.

Not long after I was discharged from the hospital, I watched an online health summit. The speaker, a network marketing professional, explained the virtue of learning the business by properly leveraging a lead system with practical steps.

After a conversation with her, I joined what I call a "network marketing business school." It was my nickname for this unique training program that provided solid building blocks for success in the network marketing industry.

I now recommend this to everyone serious about building their dream business; it is a total game-changer. I learned the hard way that network marketing is a profession with skills and a proper mindset that needs schooling and mentoring in a structured, systematic way to avoid becoming a network marketing failure statistic.

With this growing knowledge, I find myself enjoying the business-building aspect of this venture.

Business building is based on developing solid relationships and meaningful friendships. As I focus on sharing what is genuinely important to me, and what would make a profound difference in the lives of others, I find it's an attraction to those with that same interest.

It combines what they love doing together with a lucrative lifestyle business that empowers them to increase their vitality, youthfulness, and health.

It has become my dream to help other older professional women, coaches, healers, spiritual teachers, and health professionals add network marketing to their existing venture.

Apart from the fact that network marketing offers a viable income stream with residual income potential, there is just so much more. As women, we yearn for what connects us deeply with others, with ourselves, and with spirit, so through network marketing, I'm able to build a conscious tribe of like-minded individuals.

Loneliness is a growing health epidemic. Most of us, especially older women, experience changes in family structure and quality in social connection.

We crave intimacy, depth, authenticity, and a sense of deep connectedness that links heart to heart and soul to soul.

It has become my dream to throw a lifeline of hope to my sage older "womenpreneur" sisters, not only for a brighter financial future but also to create supportive communities of collaborative sisterhood.

This is where the power of sacred sisterhood circles brings healing, new dreams, and visions—when it is intimately paired with the opportunity of tangible hope within a network marketing community.

I have no more worries about age-related loneliness. Together, I am linking arms by creating meaningful relationships with others. We have the financial means to live the way we choose, and with the time available for our loved ones and finally, time to nurture our feminine essence.

Contact the Author: Geli Heimann
Email: AromaChiLife@gmail.com
Visit: www.aromachi.life

Accidentally Intentional: How we took back control

By Graham and Nikki Cheetham

Graham: Every day was the same! Nikki would go off to work at 7 a.m., and I would be vaguely aware of her leaving. I would hear our children getting ready and know that I needed to get myself out of bed to take them to school. It may seem like a straight-forward thing for someone to do, but when you have partial functional paralysis, fibromyalgia, and chronic fatigue—it is a little more—a lot more.

Nikki: Graham had suffered health issues almost as long as the 25 years we had been married. However, his health had declined significantly and for the past 22 years. He had been reliant on a walking stick, wheelchair, and numerous other aids around the home to help him with day-to-day life. Even the simplest of tasks would be exhausting for him—lifting his arms to wash his hair, tying shoelaces, cutting up food, opening jars, etc.

His day would start by driving the children to school after they had gotten themselves dressed and preparing their lunches. He would then come home to rest until it was time to fetch them from school. He would often sleep 1-2 hours during the day and could only manage minor household tasks if his health permitted. He suffered brain fog, which would often leave him unable to understand the most basic instructions and left him little in the way of thought clarity when he was feeling his worst.

Graham: It broke my heart to watch Nikki leave the house every morning, often in tears because of the exhaustion of managing a full-time teaching job and taking care of our family. But what other choice did we have? My health had left me feeling hopeless and broken. I could not support my family financially the way I wanted. I could not take part in simple activities with my children; I couldn't even play catch with them! I felt as though I had been dealt a lousy hand of cards and that nothing would ever change. This caused me to sink into a deep depression where I couldn't see anything other than my failing health.

Nikki: Many well-intentioned people had approached us over the years with the "solution" to Graham's health problems. The day he was approached to try a new "technology" that could supposedly help him was met with a less than enthusiastic response.

Graham: Imagine the scene. There I stood, walking stick in hand when a relatively new acquaintance approached me. He asked me what was wrong with me—somewhat taken aback and more than a little insulted by his frankness, I proceeded to tell him about my health challenges. He told me that he had something that could help me, something that could improve my balance, my health, and my neurological impairments without drugs. I proceeded to avoid him for two weeks! I failed to see how anything could help me, especially since medical professionals didn't know what else they could do for me.

But it did. And everything changed.

Nikki: Graham's wellness began improving once he started wearing the product. As a result, he could function better during the day, had far less fatigue, and could make it through the day without sleeping! This technology introduced us to network marketing—something we had vowed never to touch! But with such an incredible change to Graham's quality of life, we felt compelled to get involved with the business and share what we had found with others. We have found far more than ground-breaking technology, however. We have found a community of like-minded people who want to make the world a better place for themselves, their families, and their friends—a community driven by self-improvement and taking back control.

Graham: Coming into this business has given us time freedom. It has allowed Nikki to leave her full-time job and spend more quality time with our family like she desperately wanted. It has allowed me to wake up and realize that it wasn't my health holding me back all this time—it was my mindset. As a result of this, I am now inspiring others to reach for more (than they feel) their current circumstances allow. Together, we are creating a business that fits our family and hobbies and not the other way around. We have left behind the mundane 9-5 world and have found the freedom to prioritize the most important things in our life. Our children love having Nikki around more, and of course, they love that they have a dad who can be a little more active and a lot more present.

Looking to the future, we are excited to own our dream home one day, support our adult children as they venture out into the world, and inspire and encourage others to transform their lives. It doesn't get much better than that.

Contact the Authors: Nikki and Graham Cheetham
Email: accint@cheethams.uk
Visit: www.accidentallyintentional.uk

Third Time Was the Charm

By Greg Knapp

Before network marketing, by many standards, my life would have been considered rather good. I've had good-paying jobs, and I coach hockey. Although my marriage ended in divorce, I have two amazing daughters and now a granddaughter who brings me great joy and keeps me on my toes—all in all, a pretty normal life.

But something was missing. Despite being thankful for employment, I hated being an employee. I found myself subject to an employer's whims where I was little more than a line item on a budget, not a person. This was not the case with every employer I have ever worked for, but it happened often enough to cause a lot of frustration. There had to be more than this!

As a result, from my earliest working days, I gravitated towards being self-employed. In my early twenties, I worked as a driving instructor. In my thirties and forties, I worked as a contract worker in the IT field. Sure, these businesses had their frustrating times, but I loved being my own boss for the most part.

As satisfying as being self-employed was, I was still "employed." There were times when I ended up on the wrong end of the whims of a network administrator or project manager because I was "just a contractor." So, while self-employed was an improvement on merely being an employee, it was certainly not good enough.

I knew I couldn't keep living this way, but I had no idea how to get out. Owning a franchise? The thought of spending a half-million dollars on a pizza or doughnut franchise sounded like trading one form of slavery for another. Nope, that wasn't the answer either.

Network marketing first entered my vocabulary back in the '90s. I had never heard of it, and I had no idea how it was supposed to work, but it carried promises of health and wealth. Why wouldn't you want to try that, right!? Well, that first experience that died a quick, merciful death.

Fast forward to 2010, and I was approached by a friend who was building a business with a great company. It did have some appeal, so I gave it a shot, completely forgetting my earlier experiment. This time I lasted longer, with a small amount of success, but nothing that would stick. It was frustrating, to say the least. I am no longer with that company now either.

A few years later, in 2017, a good friend was sharing a product she was selling. I was curious, and since I was a good friend, I tried it out. Not bad stuff, but it didn't come across as all that earth-shattering at the time. I later realized why but that's another story. In 2020, I was off work, and with some time on my hands, I started looking into this company further, asking more questions of my friend. It didn't take long before I signed up with the company. They say the third time's the charm.

As of this writing, I have been with this company for almost a year now, and there are already many reasons to be optimistic about the future!

Would I say I have a dream life at this point? No, but it is well on its way. Life has become a lot better in the last nine months, but it's not from making money – although that will come. So, how is this better? Why does this time feel different? What I have learned is that this business is about serving. I am learning how to put my customer's needs first, ahead of my own. That's huge! I no longer bludgeon people with product and information overload. I'm learning how to talk to people about them, listen to their issues, and then help them with what they need, not what I think they need. This feels (and is) much more like me, and I like this. I really do.

The "culture" I am now immersed in is more me, too. People help one another even when there's no financial benefit. It's a little weird these days, where business is more often competitive before cooperative, but again, I like it!

Lastly, I am learning to be a leader. I have done some really cool things in the last nine months that I would have never imagined doing in the past. I have even been a speaker at a company event, which has been a great learning experience. And, just as cool? I've often thought about becoming an author through the years, but I didn't know what to write. Now, here I am! I hated being an employee. Being self-employed wasn't a whole lot better. Network marketing, however, has helped me in ways I never thought possible—and it has nothing to do with money, although I am making more now than in my first two attempts. I have learned that the best way to have a dream life with network marketing is to work on what's happening in me and let that flow outward. Here's to something more than just a pretty normal life.

Contact the Author: Greg Knapp
Email: gregknapp.29@gmail.com

GETTING MYSELF BACK

By Ibiyeye Tolulope Kawthar

Motherhood changes a woman. I, however, only understood the depths of the changes that can happen when I got married and had children myself.

I was this driven young lady who'd envision something and charge head-on for it without looking back. I was ambitious. I started my first business at 23, right out of university. I started rearing and selling chickens and made lots of profit while waiting to get admitted to a master's program. It was fun making all that money, and I knew right then that I wouldn't be hunting for a job for a very long time. It was as if God heard my wishes when I won this huge grant that I had applied for earlier, which allowed me to get my business officially registered, and I built a factory where I produced chicken feed for local farmers. I was having the time of my life doing the things I loved alongside my (then) fiancé.

Being a traditional business owner had its ups and downs, one of which was the recession that hit in late 2016, causing the price of things to increase, and many local farmers closed their businesses. I lost up to 90 percent of my customer base. So, my business, which was the only source of income I had at the time, literally went crashing down like a brick wall when it tumbled (loudly) to the floor. All this happened around the same time I gave birth to my second child – a baby boy. So, I had lots of time on my hands to rest, and various thoughts were running through my mind about what to do going forward. I thought a lot about reviving my business, but deep down, I had already given up the idea that I could make it work again.

This situation became a time of deep reflection for me. I thought back to all that I used to be and all the fire I used to have inside me. It was then that I realized that somewhere along the line, I had lost the zeal I used to have to push things through and keep chasing things that I wanted. I now found it so easy to let go of the things that used to matter to me. The things that I had worked so hard to put together just weren't as important to me as they once used to be.

I had grown by becoming a wife and a mother of two adorable little ones who made me the center of their world. I guess my subconscious had picked up that I now have three other humans to consider before making decisions concerning me and how I spend my time away from home. I had—just like a lot of moms—began putting myself, my needs, and my aspirations on the back burner. It became either the kids first or my husband first. I'll manage. Ha!

So, by March 2017, just a month after my son was born, I came across a post made by a university friend. She had so many pictures from her company events, and it was so obvious they were having fun, and everything looked super colorful. I was blown away. Now, this same friend of mine had sent me chats a year ago, asking me to look at her business opportunity, which of course, I had ignored (back then). As I was now ready, I picked up my phone, went back to her chats, read up on the business, and placed a call.

And that was how network marketing came into my world. I signed up, ordered my skincare products, and tried out the cosmetics, which I loved. It's been four years now, and I'm still in awe of the transformation that has happened to me.

Now, I know that it's the income or time freedom that appeals to many people in this industry. But, for me, it was getting myself "back." This business pushed me to reach down inside and put out that passionate and ambitious lady hiding behind motherhood.

Today, I am not only making money from the comfort of my home, and I am doing it together with a team of other women who are growing and becoming the best version of themselves through the opportunity that network marketing provides. I built a Facebook community called Crazy Ambitious Moms, where we inspire and motivate one another never to let our dreams and aspirations die simply because we have people depending on us.

Contact the Author: Ibiyeye Tolulope Kawthar
Email: teeibiyeye@yahoo.com
Visit: www.facebook.com/tkibiyeye

SECOND CHANCES

By Jan Horne

In 2001, I chose "to take the road less traveled," and left my teaching position in New York and moved to Atlanta to begin a new career as a music relaxation specialist. It was an interesting time in our world; it was right after 9/11. I was embarking on a new adventure – to create a brand-new program in a hospital with no clear direction or map to follow. As time went by, the program began to take root and grow, and soon after came a pivotal moment that changed the course of my life forever.

Fast forward to late 2010, when I experienced a very personal and painful tragedy. My youngest brother succumbed to the depths of his emotions and took his life. It was beyond devastating and very unexpected. I fell into a deep state of depression, and the sadness and emptiness were overwhelming at times. I did my best to keep "my chin up" and do my job; however, the personal toll was too much, and I took a leave of absence from the hospital. Around this time, I was approached by a family member to consider using some products from a network marketing company to support my emotional well-being.

As I continued to struggle in processing my emotions, I finally relented and said "yes," not because I believed the products would help but because I didn't have the energy to say "no." I clearly remember my first experience with the product and immediately knew that this was valuable and tangible. The effect on my emotions was undeniable; I felt tingling sensations throughout my body. Although I didn't understand what was happening, nor could I put words to what I was feeling, the experience was deeply moving and truly life changing.

Over the next year, I immersed myself in learning as much as possible. It was important to me to understand how I could support my health more naturally. As the heaviness on my heart began to release its grip, my emotions and senses reawakened. I knew I wanted to share my story and my journey back toward health and wholeness. My daily routine became more consistent, focused, and uplifting. I committed myself to live each day with a renewed sense of purpose and passion.

Through it all, network marketing allowed me to discover my "gift" of inspiring and uplifting others as they travel on their journey. My business became the vehicle to share not only my life experiences but to support my healing process. I felt compelled to let others know that it is possible to move forward and experience joy once again, even after experiencing a tragedy like losing my brother.

When my husband and I imagined all the possibilities offered to us through our business opportunity, it was then that our business grew and expanded. We now have an extended "family" with who we are privileged to share life and who are there for each other in good and not-so-good times.

Being involved in network marketing has provided us with a multitude of experiences and exciting adventures. One of the most unexpected ones came on the dance floor. My husband and I started taking dance lessons to celebrate my 50th birthday, and to our great surprise, we fell in love with competitive ballroom dancing. When we dance, we are transformed into the fullest expression of who we are. We are truly blessed to have access to incredible products that support our commitment to a healthy lifestyle. We're able to push back the hands of time and move forward, enjoying a sport well beyond when most people have hung up their dance shoes. We're so grateful for our network marketing business and this second chance to pursue (in a much greater way) our love of dance.

Who says you must give up your dream of competing at the U.S. Dance Championships? Who says you can't compete at the World Dance Championships just because you're in your retirement years? Certainly not us! We're ready to have our version of "Olympic" moments no matter how old we get.

A co-worker asked me one day, "Why would you even attempt to do something like this at your age?" My response, "Because we can!"

Just as I took a chance so many years ago when I moved to Atlanta, I now have this opportunity, this moment, to start a new adventure.

I am grateful that we choose to light the way for others so they, too, can fully express their God-given talents and for them to be true to who they are, and most importantly, be unstoppable!

Contact the Author: Jan Horne
Email: ballroomdancerjan@gmail.com

Happiness, Health & Living Life

By: Jennifer Hill

I'm a teacher and a coach – a teacher and coach who loves to travel, spoil her nephews, shop and treat herself to spa days. As you may know, this is not a profession that brings in a lot of money.

So, several years back I was looking for an opportunity that would allow me to branch out, bring in some extra income and still live an eventful, meaningful, and purposeful life. At this same time – right around my 30th birthday – I also found myself in a less than desirable situation.

I had recently suffered a serious knee injury that forced me into a wheelchair. On top of that, I was overweight. As a former collegiate athlete, I felt like a bit of a has-been. It was at that time when a network marketing opportunity came up that would not only allow me to help myself, but also to impact others. For a teacher and coach, this couldn't have fit in with my profession and personality more seamlessly.

I initially jumped on this opportunity as a way to get my life back and get my product for free. However, this quickly morphed into something much bigger once I saw what it was doing for me. I hit the ground running to help others. I knew there was no way that I was the only person in the world with these struggles. And I wanted to inspire and motivate everyone.

The next life-changing revelation came when I discovered the utter freedom network marketing allowed me. I could work from anywhere – whether it was from my phone or while on vacation, the freedom was almost limitless. And it was just amazing. I truly loved what I was doing and possessed so much passion for it, I knew I needed to reach out to others like me.

The main challenge I faced was finding people willing to admit they needed help and desired time freedom, as well. I also didn't want to offend anybody by reaching out to offer my help. I only ever came from a place of passion and love and never wanted to come across as insulting.

Luckily for me, my enthusiasm shone through. The pieces fell into place fairly easily because I was so passionate about my product and because people could see the tangible positive impact it had on me. By putting myself out there and sharing my experience, people witnessed where I'd been, where I was and where I was going – they saw my transformation occur first-hand.

When people ask me today what I'm doing or how I am, I answer, "I'm living life and I'm loving life." And this is the truth. When network marketing first appeared in my life, I was in a place where I needed to help myself. I needed to grow and conquer the struggles in myself and in my own life. Once I overcame those challenges, I was ready and excited to help others.

This passion only grew when I discovered how network marketing gives me the freedom and flexibility to create the life and lifestyle I want. I'm able to travel almost every weekend – whether it's to visit friends, family or simply to get out of town – and I can work along the way.

I also hope to stop teaching at some point in the near future. As much as I've enjoyed teaching and coaching over the past 15 years – it's really who I am as a person – my goal is to be in a position to focus on my network marketing business full-time. However, once I achieve this, I will still be able to work in an educator role.

As my business has grown, it's allowed me the ability to teach, mentor and coach others who are wanting to do what I do. I feel very blessed to live the life I live and to be in a passion-filled job that allows me to impact others.

Contact the Author: Jennifer Hill
Phone: 325-212-6946
Email:Jenafer14@icloud.com

Seeing God's Handiwork Up Close

By Jerry McLennan

Would you like to know how being recruited by the CIA led me to realize that God is always in control?

I dreamed about a job …

Do you love to fly? Do you love Ferris wheels? Does the idea of being pulled into the sky in a glider where you can soar in silence thrill you?

I once dreamed about all those things and being recruited by the CIA would allow my dreams to come true. As life would have it, God nudged me in His direction as He had done many times before. You do know He is in control, don't you? Does He nudge you, too? He's been closing and opening doors and windows gently and not so gently my entire life, reminding me that He is in control and preparing me for what's to come.

He molded me into excellence in multiple areas. My first nudge was not hearing from the CIA until after listening to Him about the husband He'd chosen for me. When the CIA offer finally came through, I knew it was not HIS plan for my life.

Instead, the plans included a series of interesting jobs from dredging the Gulf of Mexico to oilfields worldwide, being a legal secretary, running a senator's law practice, mucking horse stalls, having international competitor status, and flying horses to Europe.

Those were dream jobs. Catch my drift? Yuck job to dream job? Do you have the desire to shift yourself and soar? It's hard not to run ahead of God. He is in control. So, I learned to choose Him as my pilot, not my co-pilot. Things happened that I didn't even know I wanted to happen. It's my job to always say "yes" when God asks!

I want to share my network marketing journey with you. Trust me; it took a while. It all started when my friend, Holly, invited me to a study on oils of the Bible. In truth, she had extended this invitation many times. I wanted to go, but "life" always seemed to get in the way. It always seemed like horses needed feeding, the cows were out, or something was injured … and somehow always on the days when she would invite me to the study.

Holly never quit inviting me. Finally, another invitation came. This time, I invited a friend so I'd be accountable to someone other than myself, and it worked! I arrived early, but my hormones were raging hotter than the H.E. double hockey stick side of hot, and living in South Texas, believe me, I know about hot!

I stepped outside the home where the Bible study was being held to see if I could bring my body temperature somewhat closer to bearable to no avail. I returned to where the meeting was being held and told the presenter I might have to slip out again and why. She handed me a bottle and said, "Give this a try." Within 15 minutes, my body temperature had fallen below the triple digits it was used to, and my first thoughts were, "Wow! It's a miracle! I need to go home with some of this!"

And go home with it, I did. Hindsight is always 20/20, but it didn't take a brain surgeon to figure out that God had orchestrated the timing of the Bible study, the animals' health, and the timing of my overheating dilemma! I quickly realized God was asking me to serve others in a way that met their needs. I said "yes" to His nudge. Now I get to watch transformed lives soar as well!

And now I'm my own boss though I will always be second in command; remember, God is in control. I've traveled all over the world, taught Bible classes in the places the study talks about, met people God placed in my path to help Him meet their needs, and get closer to the abundant life He has planned for them. On top of this, I get to see His handiwork as their lives are changed forever.

Presently, my ideal audiences are women who face the aggravations of menopause, night sweats with no sleep, or husbands accusing them of extramarital affairs since they are unwilling to have sex because of pain from vaginal dryness. These women need help physically, emotionally, and sometimes financially.

The companies with whom I partner provide opportunities for me to meet people where they are, listen to their problems, minister to their pain, and see smiles on their faces when those needs are met, and their lives are changed forever.

Why? Always because God. Is. In. Control.

Contact the Author: Jerry McLennan
Email: jerrywmclennan@gmail.com
Visit: www.jerrymclennan.com

ATTITUDE OF GRATITUDE

By: Joe Pizzimenti

I hated myself. There was a time, not that far back, when I couldn't even look in the mirror. I was a gambling addict. I suffered from depression. And I attempted suicide three different times. However, both despite and thanks to the challenges I've overcome, today I live my life with an attitude of gratitude.

Rather than seeking out destructive means of escape or sinking into the darkness when tough times arise, I instead focus on gratitude and serving others. That is my greatest passion these days – providing any type of value to the world that might help even just one person. I am now living a life I couldn't even have dreamed of just one year ago.

This change in circumstances and attitude did not come overnight. Back in 2014, I spent 30 days in a rehabilitation facility for my gambling addiction and I'm currently seven years into my recovery. The time I spent in rehab provided me with the foundation and tools to start reinventing myself and my life. I scrubbed my soul and started down the path to self-improvement and growth.

The next piece of the puzzle fell into place when I discovered network marketing in 2017. I knew next to nothing about the industry when I was approached about it by a friend. And even though I'd worked in telecommunications for 20 years, I was not on the sales side. I worked with vendors and customers to ensure a smooth process on both sides.

So, entering the world of network marketing was far outside my comfort zone. However, I know we aren't guaranteed tomorrow. And with that in mind, I try to live my life to the fullest and grab any opportunity that comes my way – even if it scares me. Plus, I was drawn to the relationships I could build and maintain through network marketing, as that was my role in the telecommunications industry. And lastly, I was looking for a way to bring in some additional income that wouldn't interfere too greatly with my current job. I figured I'd just take it day by day and see what happens.

I quickly discovered that the network marketing industry is filled with people who want to make the world a better place through their products and services. However, in order to help others, you must first help yourself.

I started meeting people who supported me and pushed me to be better – which fell right in line with my mentality of striving to be the best version of myself possible. In order to make myself better so I could then serve others, I had to get out of my comfort zone even further. I had to be vulnerable. I had to tell my story and listen to the stories of others.

Before long, I hadn't simply made myself better from a business standpoint, I'd also made myself a better husband, father, and friend. I'd also started making myself better for me.

In 2018, just one year into my network marketing journey, I was laid off from my telecommunications job. Even though I hadn't been happy in my job for quite some time, it still came as a bit of a blow.

In the past, I might have turned to destructive distractions or fallen into a depression. Instead, I tackled this challenge with gratitude and positivity. I took the opportunity to sink my teeth into my network marketing business and wait to find a job I truly wanted.

The next year was the toughest of my life, but when tough moments would arise, I didn't focus inward. I focused out. Rather than throwing a pity party, I'd reach out to someone to see if I could help them in any way. I started each day by writing in my gratitude journal. And I strived to provide value and support to other people. In the end, getting laid off was a blessing in disguise. And because of the relationships I'd cultivated, I had a way to serve others which shifted focus off my own obstacles during that time.

Today, I am in a job I truly love. I'm living a life I couldn't have fathomed just a couple years ago. Network marketing has opened doors I never knew existed. I now have the privilege of working with a nonprofit that's dedicated to suicide prevention and awareness.

The CEO of this organization is one of my network marketing business partners. Because of the experiences I've had, both in life and network marketing, I'm now in a position to coach and mentor others. Knowing that I'm able to help people and impact their lives in a positive way is my greatest passion.

My ability to serve others is a direct result of the self-improvement, growth, and opportunities that network marketing has brought into my life.

Contact the Author: Joe Pizzimenti
Email: joe@attitudeofgratitudeconsulting.com
Visit: www.attitudeofgratitudeconsulting.com

THE JOURNEY OF HAPPINESS

By Johanne Pelletier

"Happiness is not a state to arrive at,
but a manner of traveling."
~ *Margaret Lee Runbeck*

It was probably somewhere about 3 or 4 in the morning. My husband, Brent, was slumbering peacefully away in the bed beside me. Little did he know, I had been struggling for a couple of hours now, my sleep interrupted by a feeling of profound panic and all that comes with it. There was the churning of thoughts, the dreaded night sweats, and most concerning of all, what felt like an inability to catch my breath. My stomach was in knots as I filled it with anxious feelings. I'd never felt this way before, and my heart was racing too.

In that moment, I was scared for myself.

In that moment, somewhere deep down, I knew that something needed to change. For a while now, I had been sitting at my desk at work, going through the motions and wondering—what am I doing here? Why do I feel this stressed?

I don't love what I'm doing. I don't feel at all like myself, and I can slowly feel myself getting further away from my life's purpose. I wanted more out of this life—and yet how can I possibly add more to my already insanely busy work and family life? What else could I do? Is it too late to learn a new skill?

That was me 15 years ago. I was a stay-at-home mom who had decided to rejoin the workforce after 12 years. I loved being home, and I felt blessed to impact our three amazing and now adult children. And yet, here I was—looking for MORE! I wanted to have financial independence again. I had a growing feeling that this was my time.

My children were at the age where they would be leaving the home Brent and I had built together in just a few years, and I wanted to find my purpose and self-fulfillment once again. In the past, I'd held various corporate finance and marketing positions as a Certified Public Accountant. I went into accounting solely because I was good with numbers, not necessarily because I was passionate about them.

As I began to look at my options, ones that would allow me to still be present in my family's life and feel a sense of accomplishment, there was an opportunity to help a friend grow her recruitment business.

At first, I was excited because everything was new. And yet, in a short time, that disturbing sleep-interrupting panic sunk in and quickly manifested into full-blown anxiety. I was confused about what I was feeling. I found myself running in that proverbial big city rat race. I had no time to enjoy life. I commuted into the city daily, getting in early and leaving late, coming home to my family, and was so busy with dinner, kids, homework, activities, etc.

Perhaps you can relate?

Stress had caught up to me. Right there, at that exact moment, I decided to leave that job and concentrate on my health. And you know what? This was the best thing that happened to me, or more precisely, for me.

I understood that I needed to slow down. And so, I took steps to explore yoga and meditation, starting my personal growth and development journey. Fate intervened, leading me down a path that ultimately blended my professional and personal goals (and skills) in the most loving of ways. This became the magical recipe for my happiness, health, and success.

I've had the privilege of representing a health and wellness network marketing company for over ten years now. Not only does this opportunity afford me the flexibility to be with my family while also earning an income, but it has also given me precious time to support my health. Today, Brent and I live in beautiful wine country, surrounded by lush nature. We have our dream home with ample space to bring family and friends in close and create lasting memories. I have ample time to prioritize my health and earn an income that supports my desire to enjoy the meaningful things in life—good food and great wine with family and friends.

Many people wish they could do something else in these challenging and uncertain times, and they're unsure of exactly what to do. Understandably, they worry about how they will meet their financial obligations with a mortgage or rent looming over their heads.

I am here to encourage you to step out of your comfort zone and try something new. Reduce your stress and feel empowered to show others the benefit of having a healthy lifestyle. Network marketing gives you both time and money, so you, too, can have it all by enjoying what you love most with your family and friends. It's time to begin to dream again.

If you are a person who, much like me, has felt the stress of everyday life and you're anxious because you want to create your dream (instead of supporting someone else's), I urge you to consider network marketing.

If you're someone who wants to feel happy, fulfilled, abundant, and positive, then you may have found the right person to help you. After all, you found this book to get you started!

I am here to tell you that there is hope. Having a plan that leverages your time is necessary so that you can follow your dreams again. There is a different way of "doing" life and getting out of the rat race. I am so grateful that I said "yes" to network marketing ten years ago. I can now be that light and hope for others to live their best life.

My invitation for you is to see the endless possibilities available to follow your passion, to become healthier, and to spend time with your loved ones while becoming the best version of yourself along the way. That is what I call true happiness!

Contact the Author: Johanne Pelletier
Email: johanne@johannepelletier.ca
Visit: www.liveintheflo.com

My Healthcare Journey

By Joni Goodmann

Working in the corporate world in the medical field was something I enjoyed; It was a privilege helping patients feel okay with what was ongoing with their health. This work gave me set hours and paid time off, although sadly, it also caused me to miss many school activities with my children. Vacations had to be planned out months beforehand to have time off from "the job."

Then, one day, my life came to an abrupt halt! Several doctor visits later, a diagnosis was finally given, although it was not one I wanted to hear—you have fibromyalgia and could be the poster person for the disorder. My doctor said I could no longer schedule time off from work because there will be zero warnings for your health. Knowing about my family's situation with my oldest son dealing with ADHD and my other son having Autism, I knew that the corporate world was no longer an option. I had to focus on my health as well as two of our sons. Our family was now one paycheck short, and more medical bills would be coming in the mail. All of this was falling upon my husband's shoulders. I felt so guilty and horrible that this financial pressure was all on him due to me not working outside the home.

Fast forward to 2012 when life t threw us a new curve ball—a car accident with four out of our family of five in the car. My condition flared up, new issues appeared, and most of our boys were injured. Being told I have "post-concussion syndrome" that probably would never heal and that the tumor in my brain grew a small bit was nothing if not alarming. Worst of all was my memories were all wiped out. I lived in a fog, ended up gaining weight, and I felt worse than before. Unfortunately, my husband was not (always) able to take off work to join us on our doctor's appointments because he had to work. This was certainly not what we needed, but what could we do with just one income? I was constantly thinking about what I could do to help our situation.

I started to follow an amazing woman who I had seen on Facebook a few times. She was on a reality show and had caught my attention as in— "Wow, look at her life!" I followed her, and one day I said, oh heck, I'm just going to message her!

You see, I had low self-esteem and wondered why this woman would want to speak to me. I was "just" a stay-at-home Mom, dealing with multiple health issues, and did not have much to share with her. We chatted, and she offered to do an NLP session with me.

It changed my life! This session was the start of a new road for my family and me. This same person introduced me to network marketing and how I can do it at home and set my hours. My health would not stop me from doing this! I said, "Yes!" Let me try this! I could help support our family with income that was needed for so many different things.

Since saying yes, learning what to do and what all that meant, I have felt much better about myself. I was able to be the mom my sons needed. Work was around my schedule, so I could be present for doctor appointments or if my son was having a rough day. Network marketing has allowed me to find gratitude and be healthy. Most of all, knowing we would have this income was taking stress off my husband. He could now pick and choose his double shifts and do what he needs to with his second job.

Knowing I was now contributing to our household uplifted me to be a new person. Being able to do home repairs and take mini vacations with the boys while not adding to the credit cards was a great feeling. I felt so much gratitude for being able to reduce my husband's overtime and the burden that had all fallen on his shoulders. Speaking to women in similar situations that we were in not all that long ago and encouraging or helping them with solutions makes me so grateful for finding out how to work from home.

In 2020 I even upped my game and focused on learning how to be even better at network marketing. I learned how to offer solutions by listening to others better. Having a team that lifts me (if I need it) helps in so many ways. Their support helps me see a better way to be both mother and wife while working from home. I am excited to see where this journey continues in 2021. All this from one Facebook connection and learning that you really can make money at home. Thanks, Mark Z!

Contact the Author: Joni Goodmann
Email: overcomingmyodds@gmail.com

LIFE CHANGES

By Karry Franks

Friday, July 18, 2014 was not only my son's birthday, but it was the day my world changed in so many ways—some for good, some for not so good.

At 6 a.m. that morning, my mom checked into the hospital. She was scheduled for two major surgeries. My request not to have them both done at the same time fell on deaf ears. She was to have her abdominal aorta, which had been damaged in a previous surgery, repaired, and the lobe of her right lower lung removed. By 3 p.m., I was notified that all went well, and she was in ICU.

I live eight hours away from my parents. I was to travel over in the next week to take care of my mom when she was released. I was a productive real estate agent and was always busy showing houses, writing contracts, and going to closings. This work afforded me the freedom to take the time to be with her while my dad worked. However, it did mean that I would always be working via phone and computer. If I was not showing houses and writing new contracts, I was not making money.

On Monday, my mom was transferred to a regular room. By Wednesday, she complained that she couldn't breathe, so she was transferred back to ICU, and I told my dad that I would be there Thursday. I got there in time to spend about an hour with her when I had to explain to her that the doctors wanted to put her on a ventilator so she could rest. She agreed, and my dad signed the consent form. I told her I loved her. Six weeks later, we had decided to take her off life support and let her be with Jesus. That was one of the hardest days of my life. My dad was devastated.

I stayed with my dad for another two weeks. My husband was so wonderful through the whole thing. When I got home, still in my fog of grief, I went straight back to work. I had buyers who wanted to see houses and sellers who wanted to sell theirs. At this point, I couldn't say that I was doing well at all; I honestly was just going through the motions. I was home for three weeks working and then back to my dad's house for a week every month for a year and a half. I was numb, depressed, exhausted, and in pain. I had not given myself the time to grieve and honestly didn't know how.

I was reading the book "Healing Oils of the Bible" by Dr. David Stewart. I wholeheartedly believe that God has designed His creation for our good. I got to wondering if there was an essential oil that would help with the pain. I had developed pain during the six weeks I was at my dad's, thinking it was the "100-year-old" mattress that I was sleeping on. It was not! I found out that back pain and discomfort can result from stress, and I believed that explained mine. So, I researched oils and found one of the pine oils that helped with my pain. Not knowing what to do, how to do it, or what to expect, I used my gut to guide me and mixed pine and almond oil in a spray bottle. I then applied it to my back, down my leg, and around my ankle 2-3 times per day. Within 48 hours, pine oil gave me relief. I was thrilled! If oil could do this with nerve and back pain, what could it do with the emotions I was having? Well, the answer is WOW!

This "experiment" was the beginning of my research into essential oils and their support of our bodies. The following year, I became a certified aromatherapist. Along the way, I was introduced to the network marketing company I now belong to. This way of working was another life change. I love sharing what God has created for our good, and with this company, I can educate people about this and know that I am introducing them to 100% pure oils with no chemicals or synthetic fillers that harm the body.

Being part of a network marketing company I love and trust has enabled me to afford the continuous trips to my dad without always working while I'm there. I don't have to be doing business, worry about a buyer going with someone else, or getting back to a closing for a paycheck. My fabulous team is there supporting me while continuing to build their businesses and wealth.

Contact the Author: Karry Franks
Email: KarryFranks@gmail.com

I Choose Freedom

By Katherine Guttierrez

All my life, I have been driven by the need to teach and serve others. I became a public high school special education teacher and taught for 33 years. Working with my students was the joy of my life, and if it weren't for that, I would have found another career. Working for the school system was another matter. I hated every minute of working for them. We had no control over anything, nor was any of our input accepted or appreciated. The day's policy was implemented, and we were expected to follow it without any guidance until the next one came along. Our creativity was squashed. We were just a body in the shop, blamed for what went wrong and expected to do it all without assistance.

I found my network marketing company online while recovering from breast cancer. My body had been ravaged by chemo and radiation, and I was looking for natural ways to help my body heal. I discovered essential oils and joined the company without ever intending to turn it into a business.

In 2014, I retired to my dream of being a full-time "RVer" and traveling this great country. Even though I enjoyed seeing the sights and making friends all over the country, I missed helping and serving others. Network marketing was the solution to meeting those needs, and making extra money was a plus. I began to build my business in 2018, sitting in my chair watching the elk drinking water from the Yellowstone River.

Network marketing represents freedom to me, the freedom I never had working in the school system. The freedom to make my dreams come true in a way that serves me best and brings me joy and happiness. I am my boss, set my hours, make my own rules, and determine how much time, energy, and effort I put in at any given time. My grandkids have a ball game, and I'm there. Nature is out my door, and I go hiking. My schedule is flexible and allows time for the most important things to me, my faith, family, fun, cooking, and sharing a meal with friends.

One of the perks of being a network marketer is that I choose who I want to work with. Are they someone I can serve and add value to, and will they add value to my life? I choose to recruit people whose beliefs and principles are similar to mine. In other words, like-minded individuals. It makes things easier and a lot more fun.

When I started my business, I built it around my values. Finally, I had the opportunity to use my gifts and talents to control my destiny. Even though I have an upline and a company with policies and procedures, I have enough control to make it my own. I am in charge. The day-to-day operation of my business is on me. Success or failure is also on me. That's freedom.

The concept of network marketing may sound very scary to you, but I think that if you're like me, you will find it rewarding. You can finally be the leader you always wanted to be. Maybe you have experienced a time when you went to your boss with a great suggestion, and it was shot down. You believed you had a better way but were never able to implement it. Now you are in charge, and you can finally put all your ideas into action and see them flourish. By encouraging your team members and accepting their ideas, you help them become better leaders. You can also guide your team members to develop ideas, suggestions, and solutions to grow their businesses. In doing this, you add value and accept support from others.

When I first started using essential oils, I didn't want the business side, just the products. Then, I discovered the business would be the vehicle I could use to help people empower themselves and become true leaders. This way of working was the dream I had when I became an educator, an unfulfilled dream until now.

Living my dream life provides the freedom to be my authentic self in life, business, and relationships. It's why I chose network marketing.

Contact the Author: Katherine Guttierrez
Email: kagu70065@yahoo.com
Visit: www.christianqueenofcajuncooking.com

Everything Happens for a Reason

By: Koriani Baptist

Slapping the snooze button again, I turned over and said to myself, "10 more minutes," but unfortunately, it was already 5:30 a.m. Crap! I felt the tension rise in my chest already. Nope, I cannot be in bed one second longer.

Upsetting my boss about my late arrival was not something I wanted to do. I quickly jumped in the shower, throw on a meaningless outfit because it didn't matter what I wore to this nanny gig—spit-up, snot, or poop on me is part of the territory. Ugh!

After years of being with a nanny agency, I was so grateful to have finally found a family with one baby, a decent salary, and full-time hours that my husband and I moved into a new apartment to celebrate! Despite my gratitude, however, I was still searching for my place in the world.

Did I want to be cleaning up poop, snot, or spit-up from someone else's child and being their maid for the rest of my life? Restless, I not only felt, but I knew that I was wasting my college degree.

Right before Christmas, I got the news that this family was expecting their second child and that grandma would be moving in, so I would be out of a job—again.

The roller coaster ride of having to rely on my employers' life changes, and the pressure of paying for rent was stressful.

I then began a nanny-share job, working for two families with two baby boys similar in age. Working 10-hour days, making baby food, and washing cloth diapers while also pregnant myself was a lot to ask. My body felt so heavy, and my emotions were so scattered; I just wanted to be in my home to prepare for my baby.

As fall ended and my January due date quickly approaching, I was told once again that I was losing my job. One family was putting their kid in childcare, and the other family couldn't afford me anymore. Devastated, stressed, and overwhelmed with this Nanny yo-yo gig, I was fed up!

Putting my hard-earned college degree to better use, I began teaching pre-school and worked with special needs students in elementary school. Finally, I was in a position that allowed my teaching gifts to grow while not having the continuous fear of being let go and being replaced with grandma or a childcare facility.

My miracle baby was so perfect and precious that I never wanted to leave her side. I told my husband that I never wanted to look after anyone else's kid again.

The years passed, and another Christmas came when my husband gave me an art set. I had no idea that I would enjoy art so much! I painted and drew, and before long, I started to sell my work at vendor shows. Having this artistic outlet from the everyday stress of teaching was such a therapeutic oasis for me. The entrepreneurial bug bit me—I just loved crafting and selling my creations!

I find that God's plans are always perfect. At one of these vendors, I first learned about the power of essential oils, and my life was never the same. I fully immersed myself in learning about essential oils. My passion for teaching was a beautiful match for network marketing. Instead of teaching children, I now teach mothers to how to have natural tools at their fingertips.

I carefully looked at the income potential of this business opportunity. With my second child's arrival, I knew that having a home-based business would give me the flexibility and ownership (of my days) that I craved. I now have no alarm clock, no traffic to fight, no office politics, or erratic employment any longer. I have freedom!

I was finally free— free to love my babies at all hours of the day, free to sleep in, free to go on hikes with my family, and perhaps best of all, I have finally found my calling by creating my brand— Wellness Coach to the Mamas.

Gathering my team of people who want to use God's healing plants to restore, heal, and make an income is truly the best job I have ever had! I am so thankful that I can "work" when I want to and that there is no limit to the amount of income I can attain. Believe it or not, part of my income will now be funding water wells in Africa!

In retrospect, my years as a nanny and a teacher were not a waste; those years prepared me to lead others in finding their purpose and improving their wellness. My passion will serve thousands now. I am so happy and grateful for network marketing— yes, I am! Amen.

Contact the Author: Koriani Baptist
Email: baptistabundance@gmail.com
Visit Keepin' It Together with Koriani on FacebooK

HELPING MYSELF TO HELP OTHERS

By: Laura Whitney Ribbins

For the past 44 years, I've had the privilege of living in paradise. I first visited Grand Cayman on vacation and fell in love – not just with the island, but also with a man. I knew I wanted to marry him. So, I returned home to Boston, told my parents my plan, packed my things and moved to paradise.

With my degree in Education in hand, I spent the first three years in Grand Cayman teaching. I had a fifth-grade classroom and taught physical education across all grade levels. Shortly after ending my teaching career within the school system, I opened a fitness and aquatics center – which I still own and run today. We offer personal training, camps for kids and teach swimming lessons. In fact, one legacy I'm most proud to know I'll leave is that I've taught nearly every child in Grand Cayman to swim.

As for my personal life, six years after moving, I married the man who first drew me to the island. Our marriage lasted for seven years before we divorced amicably and remained good friends. Then, at the age of 41, I became a single mom to my amazing son, Sam. Raising a child on my own and running a business were difficult to juggle. Looking back, my biggest regret is that I missed every one of my son's baseball games because I had to work. It wasn't an easy choice, but my business needed the income, so I had to be there. Time freedom was not a luxury I possessed.

I first started on the network marketing path simply because of the products themselves. In the beginning, I didn't look at it as a business opportunity. I just happened to stumble upon health and wellness products that I loved and was able to get them for a lower price.

At that time, my money mindset was starkly different than it is now. I didn't know how to welcome abundance. Not only that, but I also get great satisfaction in helping others and would rather give away my services for free than charge for them. I found it difficult to accept that I deserved to get paid for what I was giving. I believe it was due to this way of thinking that it took several years before I saw the potential in network marketing.

About nine years ago, I came across a product that was so amazing and such a game changer that I couldn't help but get involved. There was a bit of a learning curve at first, as I didn't really understand how to turn it into a business. However, fairly quickly into it, I ranked up a couple of times and gained a little confidence. It was then I realized the untapped potential my fitness center held – not just for my business, but in my mission to help others.

Once I combined my storefront and network marketing business, I put myself in a position to help clients on multiple levels. As we build relationships and they open up to me about their health and wellness issues, I'm now able to customize programs and suggest specific products I believe would be beneficial to them.

It wasn't until I began using network marketing to its full potential that I was able to not only grow my business and income, but also expand the positive impact on my clients.

The shift in my mindset and how I operated my business did not come overnight. It took many, many years for me to discover the value in investing in myself. I've now spent the past two years working with coaches – a mindset coach and a business coach.

I welcome abundance into my life and have come to realize that in order to be of service to others, I must first help myself. I'm able to talk about money from a strictly business standpoint – with no emotion involved. And I understand that the more money I earn, the more I can pay it forward to somebody else.

I already had a great life, but through network marketing and the tools it's provided me, I've been able to increase and enhance that life. I've made it better, bigger, and stronger. I've gained confidence and broken through unhealthy ways of thinking that held me back in the past. And most importantly, it's allowed me to give more to others and help them create a life like mine.

Contact the Author: Laura Whitney Ribbins
Email:lauraribbins@mac.com
Visit: www.fitness.ky
Find Laura Whitney Ribbins On Social Media
IG: @lauraribbins
FB: Laura Whitney Ribbins

Remember Zig Ziglar

By Len Mooney

I can still hear my grandmother's voice at the dinner table. "Grow up and go to school," she would say. "Get a good job with a good company" or "Become something important" were two of her other mantras. Her favorite choices were for me to become a doctor, a lawyer, or an engineer. As you can probably guess by now, I grew up with a family that survived the Great Depression and World War II. If you asked my mother, there were times when we barely had a pot to pee in or a window to throw it out of.

So, of course, I did what my grandmother told me—I became an electrical engineer. Out of college with a master's degree, a young wife, and a newborn baby, I moved to California and got "a good job" with a major governmental research laboratory. Baby number two came along, and all seemed to be going well.

I worked my way up the managerial ladder and became the project engineer on a large contract, and then, life intervened. Following a nasty divorce, my now ex-wife moved across the country to Georgia, leaving two small possessions behind, our children.

It became quickly apparent to me that I could not keep my job and my kids simultaneously; I had to make a choice. Because my job was s project that was a direct line item for Congress, I had zero control of my schedule. A clerk in a congressional office could call on a Friday afternoon and demand a new cost estimate by Monday morning, and we had to comply. I said farewell to my cushy, high-paying but overly restrictive government job and entered the work-from-home world.

Over the next several years, I managed to survive financially and raise my kids through various work-from-home ventures. As the years ticked by, I remarried, and my new wife's brother-in-law flew out from Chicago, drew circles on a sheet of paper, and introduced network marketing to me. I didn't really understand it (I don't think he did either), but I signed up and so began my first excursion into network marketing.

That experience in multi-level marketing (MLM) didn't work out too well. I was being mentored by someone who didn't understand the business, and I was told, "just to talk to all of my family and friends and sign 'em up." The first and most important lesson in network marketing done right is to get good mentoring from someone who knows how to do it right. Not from you broke brother-in-law.

The years ticked by, and I dabbled in several different business ventures and ultimately ended up owning a flight school. Now here is where things got interesting.

At the beginning of 2008, my flight school posted record revenues of over 5 million dollars per year. But, by the fall of 2008, the economy had collapsed. Worldwide, the airline industry lost 13 billion dollars in 2009, and flight training schools found themselves being flushed down the commode.

Between the economy and a subsequent lawsuit, I ended up discussing with a friend the merits of dumpster diving for meals.

My friend observed, "Len, you can live on the streets easy. There's plenty of food in those dumpsters behind every supermarket." Wow, I thought—from a millionaire to dumpster diving in a few short years.

But times had changed, and the internet and social media presented opportunities that had never existed before in history. So, I plunged headlong into social media. I also became determined to figure out this network marketing thing. I joined a company that teaches attraction marketing and finally found my home in the MLM space. I joined a company with a free customer acquisition model and is focused on helping customers save money on things they already do. Additionally, the company is focused on mentorship and training.

No more signing up with a broke relative and hoping for the best. I am now in a position where we have daily access to training by successful people who have made millions and more. That's what it takes—training from the best.

Network marketing offers a level playing field to anyone willing to do the work required—but it does take work, and it requires the proper mentorship. One other thing; a spirit of giving is needed. If you chase money, that's what you will get. You will continue to chase money but never quite catch enough. If you serve people, the money will come. Remember this famous quote by Zig Ziglar, "You can get everything in life you want if you will just help other people get what they want."

The secrets are loving your product, getting the proper mentorship, becoming a servant leader, and doing the work. Do this, and you can succeed in network marketing.

Contact the Author: Len Mooney
Phone: 619-488-2282
52-661-110-4493 (Mexican cell)
Email: len@lenmooney.com
Visit www.lenmooney.com
Find Len Mooney on Social Media:
www.facebook.com/len.mooney.754
www.twitter.com/workwithlen
www.linkedin.com/in/len-mooney-6813aba
www.youtube.com/channel/UC7aJul61_-opu3O1Imw4iCg

BUILDING MY LEGACY

By Liz Burhans

I was very tired of the corporate world because I didn't seem to matter as a person anymore. So, after 20 years of that nonsense, I switched to working on construction projects across the U.S., making a good income, but there was a tradeoff. I lived and worked in other states far from my family, I worked long hours six to seven days a week, and on many occasions, I did not even have time off to fly home for holidays. I missed both my kids' and grandkids' birthdays, my mom and siblings, and my friends.

When I did have time off between jobs, I felt like I didn't fit in with my family or friends anymore. You see, while I was working all those hours "making the big bucks," they lived their lives—with or without you, life goes on.

About the time I started in network marketing, my siblings and I started noticing memory loss in our mom. We questioned if this was age-related memory loss or something more. Over three years, it became clear that it was much more. At first, our mom was diagnosed with mild cognitive impairment. The following year it was moderate cognitive impairment, and the year after that, she was on the high end of moderate cognitive impairment. When we finally met with her neurologist, we (my brother, sister, and I) were told she had dementia.

If you know anything about dementia, then you know that it affects your whole family. Suffice to say, the past seven years have been the best and worst rollercoaster ride of our lives. Sad to say, we are still on it! Mom has progressed past the angry, accusatory, and hateful things she has said to us. If my mom were in her right

121

mind, she would be humiliated and ashamed of what she has said or the names she has called all of us.

But there is a valuable lesson we learned which helped us deal with "Mom" or "Jessie," depending on who was calling us that day. We quit answering the phone but would listen to her messages to determine if we should call her back. We were able to know by the tone of her voice in the voicemail which person we were going to be responding to or if we responded.

See, we split her in two— "Mom" is the loving, caring mom we had for 70 plus years, and "Jessie" is the person with dementia. If Mom called, we called her back. Most of the time, she wouldn't even remember calling us.

Enter my Network Marketing journey over six years ago, which has proven to be a struggle with ups and downs, going to events and driving to meetings two hours away to help my upline grow their business. I often had no idea what I was doing and had little guidance. I was disappointed at not getting anywhere. Growing pains are real, and the "No's" were what I was told to "get out of the way" so I could get to the "yes's.

Jumping forward to November 2020 when I saw this ad on Facebook that caught my attention about "Go for Yes," which was a five-day challenge learning the "Go for Yes" way. I thought – WOW, that sounds interesting. I clicked on it and along with this offer was another offer for a 30-day Study Group coinciding with this to learn more about not only the "Go for Yes" method but also self-development, knowing my why, and knowing my ideal audience. Who was my ideal audience, and what did I want to learn?

Network marketing is my platform to build my legacy. My dream involves building multiple small, self-contained Dementia Villages on farms. They will have sources of meat along with an enclosed greenhouse so the residents can grow their vegetables and flowers year-round. Around (or near) this village will be tiny homes for U.S.

Veterans to live in with employment opportunities in and around the Villages.

I plan to educate everyone about dementia and Alzheimer's and the caregivers who selflessly care for their loved ones at home. They will have resources and respite care made available to them. I want to be a strong advocate in our legislature for paying caregivers a decent wage because many of them have no choice and end up quitting their jobs which means they have little to no income.

This world is not prepared for the Baby Boomers who already have or will get dementia or Alzheimer's. There are not enough caring, compassionate, and educated workers, nor are there enough facilities to care for them.

Personally, I would rather see a family caregiver take care of their loved one in their own home, with all the resources available for respite care, transportation, and whatever else is needed. As you can see, I have some rather large dreams. For my family's sake, I'm glad I have a company that can support those dreams.

Contact the Author: Liz Burhans
Email: liz.burhans10@gmail.com

Dreams Change!

By Lynne-Anne Gallaway

Did someone try to sell you the dream of network marketing? That was our first exposure, and yes, we "bought" the dream. However, we also were doing our thing with building a brick-and-mortar franchise business, and I had a full-time leadership position as an Administrator/Director of Nursing in a long-term care home plus three young daughters. It sounded great, freedom and travel. So, we started.

Personal development was part of the training. It helped our network marketing business and the rest of our life as I watched my husband become more confident. However, when our upline quit, we lost interest. With the new skills we learned, we expanded the franchise business and started a real estate investment business pursuing our dream of financial freedom.

While I loved my job working with seniors and running a high-quality nursing home, it was stressful. I became ill, depressed, had lots of pain, and was not coping very well. I wasn't sleeping at night. I would wake up feeling like I had been run over by a truck (at least this is what I imagine it would feel like). Every muscle hurt. I was so stiff I could hardly get out of bed, never mind going to work. When I went to work, I would have hot packs wrapped around my wrists and shoulders to use my computer. When I came home, I crashed on the couch, unable to do much. I wasn't an enjoyable person to live with. After taking time off work and being on several medications that also didn't work, I was diagnosed with Fibromyalgia. (Finally, having a diagnosis sure didn't make me feel any better!) My doctor's comment was, "There isn't anything we can do for you. You could try meditation and vitamins." Hmmm, not exactly encouraging, right?

My daughter wanted me to try some natural health products. Since I am a nurse, and this was 19 years ago, I was very skeptical as this wasn't traditional Western medicine. Fortunately, I did try them, and wow! For the first time in five years, I had two days without pain! That started my journey to energy and wellness. These products saved my life.

So, fast forward a couple of years. I felt great, had lots of energy, still worked full-time, and truly enjoyed personal development. Our previous exposure showed us that a business only grows as much as you do. So, off we went for a weekend seminar on multiple revenue streams as we were looking for more businesses to invest in. We attended a session by a person who was teaching network marketing. He commented that if you are in a corporate job or a high-paying job, you may want to consider doing a home-based business for the tax benefits. Well, that resonated with me since a large portion of my paycheck was going for taxes.

On the way home, I talked with my husband about looking for a network marketing company that I could build. His response was, "You are already in one!"

"What do you mean? No, I am not!" I said.

"Yes, you are. The company you get your natural health products from is a network marketing company!"

Yes, it was, and I could check off the things we were told to look for in a company. It had been around for a while, it had great consumable products that did what they said they would, and the company had no debt. Great! I had a company and another beginning in network marketing!

With my upline and my daughter's help, I was able to share how these products helped me overcome pain and enjoy life again. When people saw what a difference it had made for me, they, too, wanted the same results. I am blessed that many of these people (now my friends) are still on my team after all these years. As I have switched my business online, I can still implement the strategy that has worked for our other businesses: attraction marketing.

I originally built my business so that I didn't need to spend a lot of time on it. However, I still could have a monthly income that covered all the products, travel, or education I wanted to do, and I still could continue to work full-time at the job I loved.

I found out that when I needed to help my parents, I still had a monthly check even though I wasn't actively building my business. That doesn't usually happen when you work for someone else. That is the beauty of residual income.

Eventually, when I was ready, I could retire from my day job, and now I continue to build my business and enjoy my life. Now I have new dreams – dreams of building a larger legacy of residual income for my children by helping thousands of sick people tired of being in pain and ready to enjoy their lives again.

I am so thankful that I found my networking marketing company. It has saved my life and gives hope to others. In retrospect, it has been the best business investment that we have ever made, including franchise brick and mortar, real estate investing, and working for someone else. Best of all, I love the flexibility of being able to travel and still receive money. Many different dreams can become a reality with network marketing!

Contact the Author: Lynne-Anne Gallaway
Phone: 519-384-0179
Email: lynneanne@brktel.on.ca
Visit: www.lynneanne.com

Purpose, Passion, and Prosperity

By M. Susan Patterson

Purpose has always been central to my life and well-being. Even when I didn't know enough to verbalize it, purpose was essential to my ability to move forward. Without purpose, I tend to drift along, kind of in a fog with no direction, no goals, and no motivation. Through serious illness and life-changing, traumatic events, it has remained that way. I need to have a clear vision of my purpose to live my life in any order and with any meaning.

My first great purpose in my life was and is my children. I jumped in with both feet and did everything that the experts said a good parent needs to do. I reveled in the job and got up every day happy and with anticipation. After my kids were grown and gone, I found myself without purpose, so I went back to school! I found my second great purpose in teaching, which gave me purpose and meaning. I got up every morning expecting something great to happen, and it usually did. It wasn't always easy, but it was always rewarding.

Then, another big surprise. Teaching was wonderful, but I developed what is known as teacher burnout. I retired, thinking I would have time to do all those things I had put off. It was great … for about five minutes! I was desperate for something meaningful to do. Volunteering was fulfilling, but I needed something more. And so, there I was, for the first time in my life, without any purpose or passion.

It made me sad.

So, I started to sell things on eBay. That was fun! Then, I began a little Etsy shop just for something else to do. That was exciting, too, but I wanted to do something more online. Then, when some teacher friends began asking advice, I started a life coaching "sideline." I didn't realize it, but God was handing me my next great purpose in life.

Then, I got sick. Really sick with what's called a "thyroid storm," and it was life-threatening. I had thyroid disease, which went woefully misdiagnosed, and finally, it became so bad that I nearly died. Synthetic chemical medications, about eight of them, became my routine. I was so sick that I didn't even think about natural solutions; I just got by (barely) day to day. And then I discovered (some would say, was led to) essential oils. Of course, I became interested in all kinds of holistic strategies, but it all began with essential oils.

Essential oils led me to what I later found out was called network marketing. I wanted to share my story with the world and tell everyone how essential oils can change lives. But wanting to do that and doing that are two entirely different things. I struggled along, selling a little of this and a little of that, coaching here and there. People would say things like, wow, you know so much about oils, but they didn't buy anything. I became certified in every aspect of essential oils that I could find.

Through essential oils, I found Stacey Hall and her "Go for Yes" approach. It was not a coincidence or through luck or by chance. It was the answer to many prayers to learn how to share the gifts I had been given and my yearning to make a difference. I began a learning journey and put all the pieces I had been gathering into a cohesive whole. What an eye-opening experience!

Through a refreshing new approach to network marketing, I experienced huge changes in my attitude, approach, and sales experience. Something woke up inside me, and I acted differently, spoke differently, and felt differently. I enjoyed it! Now, people began asking me questions, coming to me for advice and buying what I was selling. I didn't have to be someone I'm not.

My life has changed drastically in the last year. I have a blooming business; I also have a clear vision, a great purpose, and independence. I find myself where I wanted to be all along—financially successful, confident, healthy, and sharing my story. For the first couple of years after retiring from teaching, I was floundering. Now, I get up each day looking forward to what will happen and who I can help. And I have the power to leave a legacy for my children. What more could anyone want?

Contact the Author: Margaret Susan Patterson
Email: msusan.edgew@gmail.com

A Complete Game-Changer

By: Martha Brown

Five years ago, if someone were looking at my life, they would have thought it was full, happy, and that it couldn't get much better. For me, though, I wanted more because some things were still missing. Yes, I was clean and sober after losing everything to alcohol and drugs many years prior. Yes, I had an amazing husband, a loving family, a good-paying job in a leadership role, and we owned a beautiful home. Yet, despite all this, there was still a hole I couldn't entirely fill.

My husband and I decided to foster because we wanted to support others since we were both blessed enough to have support during hardships we had faced in our lives. We knew that not everyone else was as fortunate. We were even open to the idea of adoption if that is where the journey took us. In the long process of getting licensed for foster care, I started to realize that my priorities had changed once again. I wanted to be available for our family kids' school events appeared on my calendar, so I looked at what I wanted to do career-wise and started coaching women on a part-time basis.

Our call to foster parenting came in 2016 when we were asked if we were open to taking in a placement for a baby boy being born in April. We said yes and started to prepare. Two weeks before the due date, we received a call that he was born. Three days later, we brought him home, and after being home with him for a couple of weeks, I realized even more that I did not want to go back to the leadership role that I had for the last decade. I ended up working a part-time job outside the home and continued coaching on a part-time basis.

I tell you this because network marketing changed the way I could focus on things that were important to me. In 2016, I was at an event for mothers and spoke to someone about cleaning supplies. After doing some research, I learned that one cleaning supply company had principles and values were aligned with how I lived my life.

I wanted to provide a safe environment for my kids and help people destress. I tried the company's products myself and loved them. So, I just had to share the benefits with people around me, including my coaching clients. Over time, I found another company that also aligned with my priority of taking care of my family and myself. This company helped women change their lives by getting sober and learning healthier ways to manage their stress, make money and strengthen their relationships.

The women I work with are typically moms who are so stressed that they struggle with healthy coping mechanisms, sometimes they drink too much. Introducing them to the routines and products I use has been a game-changer for many of these women. When they realize how much they have benefitted from the products, they offer them to others. It's a way to share self-care while also taking care of their family and bring in an additional income source.

Since 2016, life has been crazy for us; like many others, we've had blessings and hardships. However, the personal benefit of being able to take care of the three kids we have now is unbelievable. During the last couple of years, we lost both my in-laws within five days of each other. Fortunately, my business allowed me to step in and take care of them for a few months just before their passing. We also moved during, and I had various health struggles. Having this business income when I could not give full attention to it was a complete game-changer. It reduced the amount of stress that I would usually have during these personally challenging times. And, during this pandemic year, having the kids home full-time would typically have crushed us financially because of the time I usually need to be a coach. Having the network marketing business was a lifesaver because I could take time off when I needed to and even plan family vacations.

The most important thing that I have found with network marketing is that it allows me to serve mothers who are stressed and sometimes turn to alcohol as a coping mechanism. Now I'm able to help them while I also take care of myself and my family. I have immense peace of mind knowing that when an emergency arises—such as my kids or husband needing me, my schedule going off the rails, or when I need to slow down—I still have an income coming in, a reality that still amazes me. Now, I sleep better at night and don't put that much pressure on myself when unexpected things arise, which so often has been the case during the last year.

My dream life of focusing on what is important to me while seeing the difference it has made for my family and me (and those around me) has only been possible through network marketing.

Contact the Author: Martha Brown
Email: martha@marthabrowncoaching.com
Visit www.marthabrowncoaching.com

Removing Imposter Syndrome from My Life

By Monica W. Wanner

I'm a personable, likable, and fun person to be with. I'll bet that we'd have a great time on Zoom over a cup of coffee, where we would laugh, and you would feel at ease while exchanging experiences and stories, and as we say our goodbyes, we would both echo the words, "We need to do this again soon!"

I have a secret – in the past, the laugh was hollow, and the smile was not real. I would hide my self-doubt in my jacket pocket, place my confidence into my briefcase, and practice my smile in the elevator reflections while riding down to the parking garage. Failed or rejected. Again, and again.

I would keep trying with a new task, another project, or a challenging assignment, each time more determined than the last. And each time, I became better at pasting on my smile that I could now easily pull out of my wallet. Sure, there were lots of wins, many successes, and great income opportunities. Despite this, I was still feeling like something important was missing – where were the fun and the happiness that I craved?

Are you like me? Are you searching for something that is missing from your life? Are you trying something new and starting over? Perhaps looking for your big win this time?

Like many of you, I've started over several times. Starting over isn't always fun, and it's certainly not very inspiring or invigorating, especially when you are focusing on the hardships and challenges you've gone through. Starting over can be quite the downer, especially when you are picking yourself up and comparing yourself to someone else, as this tends to highlight your flaws and mistakes. There was always someone better than me in my journey, someone smarter and brighter, someone more likable, or more personality. In short, my comparisons with others only served to amplify my shortcomings ... gosh, if I could just be more like her, right?

And that is how I felt for many years. I was taught to duplicate and attract like-minded people to make the sale, win the contract, or ace the presentation. Yet even in times of achievement, I somehow didn't belong ... I had "Imposter Syndrome!" I understood the words and the language but didn't quite get the meaning.

Things just didn't fit right. It was like holding that last piece of a jigsaw puzzle piece in my hand and knowing exactly how to place it into that space, yet my piece's color and the pattern weren't a match for the hole staring back at me.

I wasn't learning. I wasn't smiling. And I most certainly wasn't having fun.

Fast forward to 2021, where my mindset is different. I now believe in (and have confidence in) myself. I know that the multiple failed attempts, numerous times of starting over, and comparing myself to others also had their advantages. They were valuable learning experiences that I have added to my portfolio.

I learned that I needed to have fun. I learned resilience. I learned that I could attract people. I learned that I could provide value to people, and most importantly, I learned that I was happiest when I was helping someone else!

Not long ago, after leaving the corporate world and academia, I embarked on my current network marketing adventure when I understood myself, my goals, my desires, and most important of all, my raison d'etre. Plus, I now had another advantage—my mindset! The thoughts you think and the words you tell yourself are the keys to unlocking your success. All the experiences that I had gone through gave me a better understanding of myself and how I could serve others. And that is what makes me smile today and makes me happy.

My journey in network marketing has provided me so much, especially with TIME ... time to live like I want to, time with my family and friends, time to learn, time to be healthier, and, most importantly, time to help and serve others!

Do not think for a minute that my life is perfect – gosh, far from it! I'm not a millionaire; I don't have a fancy boat at the marina, nor do I entertain celebrities in my downtown condo or on my private Caribbean island.

I am just like you. I have days when my mind still messes with me, questioning whether I made the right decision, or my smile droops a wee bit. But the difference now is my mindset – I know that everything is "figureoutable" because I am now living my life the best possible way that I can—and on my terms, I have fun and have a purpose. I am not trying to become a person of great financial success, but rather, a person of value – and that's what makes me feel that my puzzle piece fits and completes my picture!

The world needs what I have to offer. I am good at what I do, and I get paid to do what I love doing. What makes this different from previous career choices is that I have linked arms with a leadership team that an inspiring owner leads to help 1 billion people improve their health and well-being. I am so blessed and honored to be a part of this culture. It allows me to associate with so many servant leaders with big, beautiful hearts, all with the same desire to lift other people and watch them become better every day. That's how I fit in, what excites me and what makes me smile!

There is clear meaning in Sir Richard Branson's words, "to have fun in my journey through life and learn from my mistakes." Leading from my heart, I unapologetically choose my happiness over anything else! As a result, I've begun attracting more people like me – positive, happy, adventurous people who also wanted to make things better for those around them.

So, are you ready to have a bit of fun and have that virtual coffee with me now? Just say when.

Contact the Author: Monica W. Wanner
Email:monica_wanner@yahoo.ca
www.facebook.com/monicaw

THRIVING THROUGH COVID-19

By: Monika Greczek

Over the past year, throughout the Covid-19 pandemic, salons have taken a massive hit. Six shut down permanently in my area alone. As a stylist, massage therapist and salon owner, the coronavirus, and its subsequent lockdowns, forced me to think outside the box.

As so many people and businesses struggled during this time, I've been able to not only maintain my business and client relationships, but also develop additional opportunities, build new connections and provide support to others – thanks to the tools and lessons I've learned through network marketing.

I first entered the network marketing sphere back in 2010 when my coach and mentor introduced me to an opportunity. At the time, I was working ten hours a day and had a family at home – I simply didn't have the time or ability to start a second business. I did, however, use the products. And little by little, over time, I began getting more involved and picked up marketing tools and knowledge I could apply to my salon and spa.

I first became a better listener and began to fully understand what my clients were telling me. I started having more meaningful conversations and building deeper relationships with my clients. This was especially true in the area of massage therapy.

Based on what I was hearing, I started to learn more about pain and pain points. And as people told me what they needed; I could then find ways to help them through my network marketing products. It's a wonderful feeling to provide support and relief to others – but you can only do this if you're really listening when people tell you their needs.

Acting on the marketing tools I'd picked up, I decided to utilize social media to broaden my connection to others. Until recently, my I'd only ever used Facebook as a way to stay in touch with family or old friends from school. However, once I started looking at is as a marketing tool, my network expanded and my impact on others grew. We all know what a struggle this past year has been and the stress it has brought with it.

However, I've been able to stay in touch with my clients and provide advice and products to help them cope. As I listened to what issues they were experiencing, I realized there was an opportunity for me to develop my own line of CBD products to help with stress-induced problems. This is an endeavor I never would have attempted before. However, I listened, I understood, and I realized there was a real need. So, I acted. And through this, I've not only been able to expand my own business and add an additional source of income, but I've been able to further enhance peoples' lives and well-being.

As I figured out ways to use social media as a way to help strengthen existing relationships, I also built new ones. I've been able to connect with other stylists struggling during these difficult times and teach them the things I've learned. I'm now in a position where people come to me seeking advice, guidance and support.

Because of the skills and experience I've gained through my network marketing training, I'm actually able to give them what they need. It's a truly incredible feeling to know I can be of service to others in need of a helping hand.

For so many, this past year has been a matter of survival. Watching professionals in my industry lose clients or forced to close their salons, I feel very grateful for the tools and lessons I've learned that allowed my business to keep moving forward.

As of today, my salon is thriving, my CBD line is growing, and my network marketing businesses are expanding. I've always loved what I do, but I see now that I was starting to lose my passion for it. However, since finding ways to broaden my scope and increase my value to others, the spark has returned. And with it, there is more fluidity in my life. I feel freer. And now I have the confidence and the proof that I am in a position to weather any storm.

Contact the Author: Monika Greczek
Email: extasyhair@comcast.net
Visit: www.extasyhairstudio.com

Saying Yes Gives You More Options

By Patricia Daigle

Many of us don't have the opportunity to choose the path for our future. Some are born destined to be in careers or lives, others are guided (or misguided) by friends or family, or others have their future determined by various actions they take or their living environment.

I grew up in a coastal town in New Jersey. I had dreams and aspirations of traveling the world after high school. I did not have the skillset I needed to succeed at anything in particular so I was stuck in dead-end jobs at a bowling alley and a restaurant supply company. I knew there was more for me, but I did not know how to get it.

Where did I end up? At the military recruiting station where I joined the U.S. Air Force. I spent the next 20 years of my life following "the regulated" life. It was there I gained a skill set that took me through the rest of my career. Little did I realize it would also be an opportunity to travel and see places I would have otherwise never seen. I was offered a job in contract management which landed me several good positions after my military retirement.

While in the military, I became a mother of a beautiful daughter. Money was tight when it came to supporting my child and paying for daycare because I was a single parent. I was invited to a party where a woman shared all these wonderful, educational toys and books for children. I wanted all of them and was told the best and least expensive way to get what I wanted was to become a consultant and do what she was doing. This was my first introduction to network marketing. I asked, "How do I sign up?" This "adventure" gave me the funds I needed for daycare and the toys my daughter played with. By the way, my grandchildren are still playing with some of them.

Eventually, I was moved to a new duty station. The beauty of network marketing is that you can work it from anywhere. As my daughter outgrew her toys, I no longer needed this business. What I still needed, however, was extra income and to decorate my new home. Along came a friend who invited me to another party. Home décor was just what I needed for our new living space. The words, "How do I sign up?" rolled off my tongue. I wanted so many of these products. Yes, I was now sharing home décor and still have some of these products in my home today too.

Are you getting the picture by now? I started these businesses based on my wants and needs at the time. Did I know where network marketing was going to take me? Sure, I learned the income potential and the lifestyle that network marketing can create and that my "dream" life of traveling and charitable giving could become real. It just didn't then.

I moved on to my next duty station, where I met the (current) man in my life and got married. Some friends were having a group of people over for a business meeting. The adventuresome person that I am said, "We will be there." After hearing their compensation plan and meeting the people in this organization, we signed up for another opportunity. This time it was for nutrition and home care products. It was here that I started to learn about the power of personal growth and leadership. It was the first business where I attended a conference. It was there that I saw the vision of what a future in network marketing could be. A supportive community, friends who would help me learn what I needed to do, weekly meetings to gain business knowledge, always meeting new people, and the travel I had hoped for. We still use some of these products to this day and remain friends with many in that community.

Was there another opportunity that would fall into my lap? Yes! I was at work one day when a co-worker had a delivery of skincare products from her consultant. I was invited to try the products at a home demonstration. I did not have a skincare regiment, nor did I know much about creating one. This became my next learning endeavor. Once again, I fell in love with the excitement of the conventions, the training, the community, the extra income, and the home office tax benefits helped as well. I was making enough money to take a vacation each year. I met so many new friends, gained hundreds of customers, and loved the products. This business was my home for 17 years. One day another friend invited me to her home to check out a business her husband started her in. You can't let a friend down, right? So, I went to her house for a mud facial.

By this time, I was slowly losing business in the business I had been involved with for almost two decades because I was not growing personally, and the compensation plan had been revised. Was it time to change? Yes! My husband and I joined this one together. It was relatively new, with less than five years of being in business. Despite this, it had a world-class customer experience and products that were being sold in 40+ countries. Once again, I fell in love with the products. At the first convention I attended, I met the CEO, who was one of the humblest men you would ever want to meet. His vision is inspiring, and he gave our community much hope. I knew that I had a lot of personal growth ahead of me to make it to the "rank" I wanted to be. This was another new journey, so I started following the leaders, read their books, listened to their training, and absorbed their vision about this opportunity.

I retired from the military at the age of 60 but was not ready to retire from working. My vision and dream became clearer. Thanks to the conferences and training, I was starting to change and grow personally. If I wanted to grow a healthy business, I had to learn to be a team leader, increase my skill set, and teach others how to grow. I tried a couple of different training programs and found one that resonated with me. This is where I realized things could be different this time. Technology had changed so much since I first started in network marketing that it was necessary to invest in myself (even more) to move ahead.

The company I am affiliated with now offers the lifestyle, travel, and training opportunities I have dreamed about. Combined with the technology and mentorship I'm receiving; I see life with a new perspective. I get to be with people who have the same dreams, desires, and motivation. It took me quite some time, but I finally understood the entire concept of network marketing. It's not just a method of moving products or services but a way to provide solutions to various problems for both the buyer and the seller. Both sides of the table need to be open to finding answers. This long network marketing journey created a better life for my family and me—at every turn I made. It's been well worth it.

Contact the Author: Patricia Daigle
Email: yourdailynourishment@gmail.com
Visit www.yourdailynourishment.com/offer

When You Speak to the Universe, It Listens

By: Rachel Rideout

I tried my hand at online business two separate times before with very little to show for it. I hadn't seen the results I'd hoped – I hadn't earned as much money as I'd expected, I spent years as a follower, and I realized that most people liked me only because I made them money. I was done. I swore up and down I'd never sell another lotion, potion or pill again.

This was a little under five years ago and also happened to be the lowest point in my life. I was literally that person sitting on the bathroom floor crying. Sometimes I held a drink in one hand and pills in the other, contemplating doing something extreme. My full-time job was horrible, my co-workers were making my life miserable and I was in a deep, dark hole.

Then I caught a break – some friends and I went on a cruise and I was free from my daily struggles for two weeks. While sitting on the deck of the cruise ship, I suddenly could visualize the life I truly wanted. I got a taste of time freedom and realized that's what I desired. With this in mind, I spoke to the universe. And it answered.

Less than two weeks after I returned home from my trip, a friend called me with a business opportunity.

"I'm not selling any more lotions, potions or pills," I told him, but he assured me this was different. After looking over the business plan, I discovered he was right. I was impressed and something inside urged me to give it a try. For the past four years, since joining his company, my progress has been gradual but consistent. I can actually see results – not just in my business, but within myself. My mindset has completely shifted away from limiting beliefs.

In the past, I was full of all the excuses you hear – I don't have time, I can't, this didn't work for me in the past. However, along my journey, I realized that happiness and determination are choices. I decided to no longer give into my depression or less-than-desirable circumstances. Rather, I now use the tools network marketing has given me to face my challenges, think outside the box and go after what I want.

I've gained the confidence to speak up for myself when necessary and stop allowing toxic people or situations to hold me back or keep me from pursuing my goals.

I now possess the knowledge and experience to be in a position to reinvent myself. This is one of the wonderful opportunities network marketing provides – the ability to seek out different paths that best match your strengths and personality. Due to the skills I've acquired, and my shift in mindset, I'm now in a leadership role. I give presentations, assist in training sessions and currently work alongside the CEO of my company in building the business.

Not only has my status elevated thanks to the growth and development I've achieved along the way, but I've also gained credibility. If you'd told me just five years ago that this would be my life today, I never would have believed it.

Network marketing gives hope that your dream is achievable. Then it takes it a step further and gives you the tools to make it a reality. I still have my days that are more of a struggle – but that's just life. Even on those days, I utilize my new mindset to make a choice to be happy, to be grateful and to be hopeful. I ask myself if I want my life to change or just remain the same.

With that in mind, I remind myself that I need to believe in the dream, be consistent and if something isn't working, find someone who can guide me. And for the past four years, this strategy has served me well and shown me just how much is truly possible.

Contact the Author: Rachel Rideout
Email: rideout2success@gmail.com
Visit: www.rideout2success.com

BELIEVING BIGGER

By Rebekah Cole

Believing bigger was something I never thought was possible for me, just an average person. I have a full-time job, I am a wife, I am a mother, I teach Sunday School, and I am choir director. I work my 9 to 5 job, cook dinner, help with the kid's homework, do daily chores, and maybe watch TV for an hour or so before I go to bed. All in all, a typical mother's life. Do I love all that I do in my life? Yes, with my whole heart. I wouldn't change a thing because I genuinely believe that I was created for that purpose!

Despite that assuredness, somehow, all it took was a former student of mine sharing her life with me and the "possible life" I could envision for my family for that to change. At that time, I didn't even know what it would do for my health and my family's life. One day all that changed, and my real purpose became BIGGER.

On a fall evening in September 2018, I reunited with one of my former students, Denise, at Starbucks. As I was driving there, I felt this sense of peace come over me. At that time, I didn't realize what that meant. As I was walking in, I saw her smiling face and enjoyed the huge hug that followed. As I sat down and shared her network marketing journey (much like I am writing now) with the smell of chai tea in the air, I felt goosebumps.

I thought to myself—I could do this! All these thoughts came to mind about how I could start to take care of my health, my family's health, change lives, make a difference, have financial freedom, and create a life that I could never even imagine before this coffee shop experience.

At first, I thought to myself, "No way! Am I worthy enough? Am I good enough to do this? Will I understand everything to fulfill this calling in my life? Do I believe that I was created for a bigger purpose? All these different emotions and thoughts flowed through my mind that evening. As we ended our time together and caught each other up on the last 10 years of our lives, I felt a sense of hope upon leaving. This hope was nothing like I had ever felt before.

I hurried home and shared what I learned with my husband, Ben. He saw my heart and what I wanted to envision for our family. But, figuring out how to afford this next initial investment was puzzling. We knew if it was supposed to happen, then it would. The next day, Ben came home and handed me the money. The heart of my husband—who believed bigger for me and my dreams—sold his baseball cards so I could start my new journey! I had tears in my eyes; I couldn't believe it. I was so excited, and I was blessed beyond words and even more at peace than I could believe bigger in my calling. This was only the beginning of the incredible journey that was ahead of me.

What I didn't know was going to happen was that I could make an impact on a little community of mine that is near and dear to my heart. In the next five months after I started my journey to change lives, 15 deaf people joined me on this adventure—a community that I believed had a greater purpose for themselves and their family! Just watching them grow and succeed is such a beautiful thing; they have become a blessing to so many people!

I want them to love who they are in this world, know that they can do anything, and believe in a bigger purpose beyond what they first imagined when they took a step of faith forward. I have incredible people on this journey that I never imagined, my deaf friends, my hearing family and friends, and new people I get to grow relationships with that I would have never met otherwise. I love the greater purpose that manifests when we are part of a thriving community of like-minded people—the deaf inspire the hearing, and the hearing encourage the deaf. This is something I am so excited to be a part of—can you tell?

In August 2020, I met an incredible lady named Elisa, who became a mentor of mine as my journey continued. Mentoring grew my confidence, even more, helped me step out of my comfort zone, provided the "how to" for what I was doing. Along the way, she became a great friend and took my passion for changing lives to the next level—much more than I could have ever imagined! I am forever grateful for the people who believe in me and saw a greater purpose (in me) that I couldn't see myself. Thank you, Denise, Elisa, Rae, Lisa, Laura, my husband Ben, family, and friends for helping me see I could believe BIGGER!

Contact the Author: Rebekah Cole
Email: Colepig@gmail.com
Visit: www.facebook.com
groups/133796278625449

Plan Ahead for Your Retirement

By Shirleen Sando

If you're like me, you have your share of excuses. While I earned two graduate degrees and currently work at a great job, I questioned my ability to dig in and create a legacy for myself, a financial empire. That thinking was an excuse I told myself to keep from putting in the needed work.

Oh yes, I had degrees, but I also knew that my job would never give me the financial legacy I wanted, not only for myself but also for my family, others, and the animals I volunteer to help. It all takes money. To earn more beyond my retirement income, I researched network marketing and have not looked back since. I decided it was time to push the excuses away and focus on my goals and dreams.

Oh sure, those old excuses still crept into my head. And, I had plenty of doubt. Was I productive enough to build a business on the side? I toyed with the idea, played with the idea, and discovered much that I needed to learn. I pushed on. I was in it to win it.

My journey took me down many paths. One of the first things I learned was that I needed to work on myself—what a shocker! I spent years in college completing graduate work and taught many years on the university level, yet I still needed to work on myself!

I realized that if I seriously wished to build an online network marketing business, I must spend time in personal development on growing a positive mindset. I studied the law of attraction and read most of the books on the top network marketer's list. Over time, my confidence grew. I knew I could be a successful network marketer. The only stumbling block for me, and if you choose this path, is not taking action… choosing not to do the work and being inconsistent.

In many ways, I was blessed because I had a vision. I also knew I wanted to work at a rewarding job that paid, even after retirement. I wanted to build a legacy.

I am thankful that I chose to work on my retirement goals years before retirement. I see many who face retirement with the realization that they weren't financially prepared. Those goals of more time to travel to spend time with my grandchildren were lost dreams. The extra money just wasn't there.

Don't wait too long to evaluate your savings. You need enough money to adequately fund yourself for potentially 25-40 plus retirement years. If you need to build additional retirement income, start working on it today. Don't let age be an excuse. Plug in, dig in and go for your dreams.

Besides needing extra funds during our golden years, other concerns are on people's minds. We live in a rapidly changing environment, and many must supplement their income or replace lost income. Millions need to replace lost work and desire more security. For those, this might be the best time to be involved in the network marketing world. I want to secure my financial future in smart and positive ways and imagine you do too, or you wouldn't be reading this book.

Network marketing on social media is far better than it used to be. We have moved beyond building our business by holding house parties, setting up public meetings, and contacting friends and family via phone or email. While many have built large organizations that way, it is far too much work for most of us. I did build a team that way and never missed receiving a network marketing paycheck for over thirteen years. Despite the extra income, the work was time-consuming, involved travel, and took up most of my weekend. It wasn't for me.

I am thankful for the new era of social media marketing, for it has changed the face of how network marketer's work. With billions of people online, it is easy to connect with people from around the world without leaving the comfort of your home.

The world has changed with more than just the advent of social media. In 2020, the world turned upside down. Without warning, many found themselves out of work while others faced reduced work hours. People globally turned to online opportunities in droves to supplement their income, replace their income, or increase their financial security.

With modern technology on our side, with concepts such as Artificial Intelligence (AI) on the rise, we have moved into a new age, with a new energy and what I consider to be the golden age of network marketing. The world is changing. Change with it. As old technologies fade, new ones emerge. It is an exciting time to be in this space.

Whether you are working full-time or part-time, or if you are already retired, you have an opportunity to build an online community by working after work hours, on weekends, or full-time. While growing your business, listen to experts, put your work clothes on, put your head down, work on personal development, and get to work.

My involvement in network marketing has helped me find a "retirement career" that I will enjoy. Being active and engaged is something I value in life. The social connection and the sense of belonging to a supportive community offering top leadership training fill me with joy and a sense of belonging. I am involved with those who have the same goals and ambitions as I do. We train and plan, all while having fun.

Please contact me to find out more information. I am here to share what I have learned and being of service to others is essential to me. Whatever you decide to do, I wish blessings to you and your family.

Contact the Author: Shirleen Sando
Email: rssando@yahoo.com
Visit: www.thesoutherngalshow.com

The Best Decision I Ever Made

By Sigrid McNab

I'll never forget the day I first saw them. They were so tiny, precious, and sweet. Family is everything to me. Ever since I was a little girl, I dreamed of having children and of the love we would give and receive. My husband and I got married at a young age, and soon we were ready to start a family, but it was not to be. After numerous challenges, it was strongly suggested that I no longer try for the sake of my health. Fortunately, we just knew that we would receive a miracle somehow, and we did.

We traveled to Romania and adopted our beautiful baby boy and baby girl. They were so precious, and the love I felt for them enveloped my body and soul. They had such sweet smiles. I touched their tiny fingers and toes, and my heart melted. I was a supervisor in a busy hospital's microbiology department, and my husband and I also had other businesses. I loved working at the hospital, but it was also a lot of responsibility, stress, and long hours. However, it didn't take us long to realize that we hadn't brought our precious babies home to leave them in daycare.

Being home with my family and being able to provide for them was my number one priority. So, I started looking at other alternatives for making money. It was tough. Every "job" I looked at had, you guessed it, specific hours of work and few breaks. Both children had some health challenges with lots of medical appointments, so that was just not going to work.

A dear friend of mine suggested network marketing. I'd never even heard of it before, but the more I looked into it, the more excited I got! It seemed like it would meet my top two priorities:

- Being able to stay at home to look after my kids and make sure they had what they needed.
- Having peace of mind when my head hit the pillow at night because I would make some money too.

And yes! There was flexibility.

Could I create my hours? Yes!

Could I block out the important things in my life and work around them? Yes!

Could I not worry about asking permission from a boss for medical appointments, school functions, Cubs, and gymnastics? Yes!

"Really?" I asked my friend. "Tell me more!"

Joining the network marketing profession was the best decision I ever made because it works so well for my family. I could design a professional life fitting around my family instead of adjusting my entire life to fulfill my function at my job. This is one of the things about network marketing that I appreciate the most. I can be the 24-hour-a-day caregiver that my now-adult child needs without stress for us both. I am there, at home, where I want and need to be.

Network marketing can be rewarding financially. Everyone can use extra cash; it's up to you to set the limit as high as you want to go. Maybe you want money to pay a bill or to make ends meet or provide some extra things for your kids or to travel or whatever you want to do. I needed to have peace of mind financially. It helped me pay the costs of frequent travel for medical reasons and pay the extremely high prescription costs every month that one of my children still requires.

Network marketing helped me be an entrepreneur. I have met so many wonderful people who are just like me who want to stay home with their kids and dream of a better life. We want to retire with enough money or travel without stressing over our finances. One of the greatest rewards of building my business is the friendships I've made and the relationships I've built. You are not in this alone. You are part of a team, and people will help you, guide you and be there for you. When you genuinely have a heart for helping people, the network marketing industry allows you to do just that. I've been able to help people pay their bills, make a mortgage payment, buy their kids new school clothes, travel, and more—all those things that their budget just didn't allow before we met.

I'll never forget one mom. She was in tears as we talked for the first time. She wailed, "My baby is screaming. I just used my last can of formula, and I have twenty-five cents!" My heart just broke. I was so happy to help her improve her life.

I want to convey what is in my heart. This is my journey and how I'm doing my life. Everyone is going to be different, and that's okay. The secret is to believe in yourself.

Ask yourself: What do I really want? What is important to me, deep down in my belly and in my heart?

Am I going to achieve that by doing what I'm doing right now? If not, then, how will I?

I wish you much joy, love, and success in your life. I care about you even if I haven't met you yet. If you want to learn more about my specific company, or if I can help you in any way, please contact me directly. I'd love to get to know you.

Contact the Author: Sigrid McNab
Email: Sigridmcnab@gmail.com
Visit: www.sigridmcnab.com/home
www.facebook.com/McNabSigrid

THRIVING, NOT JUST SURVIVING

By Sonya Janisse

I describe myself as a retired, passive-aggressive people pleaser who has spent most of her working life in Corporate Canada while raising a family. My time, energy, and attention were always split, and I struggled to find a work/life balance. I was on autopilot, going through the motions while knowing that there had to be something better. I longed for deeper connections, real conversations, time freedom, balanced energy, and elevated finances. Most importantly, I couldn't envision my future self in this environment any longer. I needed to find a new way forward.

That was when a friend introduced me to network marketing. I should say reintroduced as network marketing has been around for ages and has become the new wave in this ever-changing and expanding internet-based society. It might look a bit different today, but the feeling is the same. I remember going to "parties" with my mom and loving it. I was finally old enough to be included with the grownups for a lady's night. Just like when I was a kid, I still look forward to that time together with friends and family. The amazing conversations, the presenter, the sampling, and the chance to explore new products and the food and laughter provide the times to connect us and create memories.

Once I was reintroduced to network marketing, almost everything changed. Instead of being overwhelmed by my future, I was jumping out of bed, eager to get my day started. I was choosing the right food (and movement) for a positive mindset. My priorities shifted from worrying about paying the bills to making each moment matter. I was thriving and no longer just surviving. I developed a fresh perspective on controlling my financial future and my time, rather than just trading time for money.

My network marketing company grows exponentially every week. Whether I'm using it through my network marketing side business, life coaching, personal training, and nutrition coaching services—it's all a part of assisting people with upgrading and elevating their life. It's a way to help people (like you) to grow and glow.

Network marketing has allowed me to live my dream life... I'm no longer a prisoner of active income. My financial portfolio has expanded to include both residual and passive income. A small investment has led to massive growth in the quality of my life. I'm proud to say that I'm a paid problem solver in a professional development industry with a sweet compensation plan. With a job description like this, "Friendly company seeks enthusiastic individuals who love helping people and are willing to learn. Life experience is a plus. Work whenever and wherever you want," I said, "Sign me up!!"

The tools to help you down this road are accessible and freely given. Your network marketing group will provide encouragement, support, and acknowledgment. Personal growth and development are strongly encouraged. The stresses of a workplace environment don't apply. Harassment, insane deadlines, evaluations, cattiness, or competition for favor are not part of the network marketing environment. The person who approached you about network marketing saw something in you. They could see your potential and believe in you. One of the best parts—not working on anyone else's schedule or waiting for a pay raise.

Think of the freedom from commuting, dress codes, fear of layoffs, or discrimination. Think of the freedom to spend quality time with those you love and to set your own goals. Think about what you can accomplish and what you can do to help others. Helping others has always been at the top of my list, and the ripple effect that comes from that is way beyond what you realize.

The best advice I can give you? Find your passion. I found mine in helping people let go of their past negativity and begin seeing themselves in a positive (and energized way), so they can begin to lead their best lives. I chose companies and products that I love because it is an extension of me and what I do. For me, network marketing is about sharing the things I love with people I believe will love them. It's about offering a quality, safe and affordable choice that benefits us both. It's about allowing me the freedom to chase my dreams while helping others to chase theirs. I can be me, and you can be you!

Contact the Author: Sonya Janisse
Email: Sonya@freshapproachfitness.ca
Visit www.freshapproachfitness.ca

My "There Has to be a Different Way" Story

By Stephanie Y. Oden

I am a wife, mom, process improvement engineer, and I now have a successful network marketing business. But I started as an ordinary girl with a good job.

I got my dream job in engineering after graduating with a degree in electrical engineering. I was considered successful by most standards—I had a husband, two kids, two cats, one dog, a company car, and a six-figure income. I was successful in all the ways that others could see. But what people couldn't see was the constant sick feeling in the pit of my stomach, not being able to sleep, and feeling like I was "off." I felt like I had lost myself in all these "things" and had the feeling that I was not really in my life, but rather that I was sitting on the sidelines of it.

I don't have a "flat broke" story. But I do have a "work-too-many-hours while stressed and overwhelmed" story. I do have a "limited in growth and opportunity if you don't want to sacrifice your family" story. And I had a "there has to be a different way" story.

When the market shifted in 2008, I was downsized. My six-figure income was reduced to a $58K annual salary with a commute. My husband was also let go from his job. I had a freshman daughter in college, and my son was still in high school. It was hard, real hard. I was so close to losing hope. Granted, we were not destitute by any means, but still, I resolved that I never wanted to be in that position again.

As I recognized the need to have an additional income source, I decided to open a brick-and-mortar business as a health and wellness service provider using knowledge and training, I had learned as part of my journey to improve my health. That was a great plan, except I broke my ankle two months after opening, and I couldn't physically provide the services and still had overhead expenses to boot. I had to rethink my thoughts about an additional source of income. That's when I decided to look at networking marketing and become a professional in the industry. I had to "unlearn" what I thought about having a network marketing business and embrace the industry as a legitimate way to earn extra income. Not only are there products to enhance my family's wellness, but there is no lid on personal growth or an income-earning cap.

My network marketing company's compensation plan does not care about seniority, favorites, or too many people achieving their next promotion in a month. You do the work—you help others be successful—you will be rewarded based on those results. All the things I enjoyed about helping my corporate team grow (and succeed) as leaders I have in network marketing.

I believe that everyone should have control over their financial destiny and that everyone should enjoy more of the things that give their life purpose and meaning. The network marketing industry and the company I am a brand partner with allow me to realize both these ideals. The dreams I realized started as just a way to afford dinner at a fancy restaurant and not have to split a meal. Next, we were able to afford a healthier lifestyle and tackle college expenses. We can now do "the extras," like when something breaks unexpectantly, we can fix it right then or enjoy some pretty nice first-class vacations without the additional financial burden. And it is a complete pleasure to provide financial support to causes that matter to me.

Whether you are struggling to pay bills, in a career transition, want to pay for your kid's activities, or want to take a much-needed vacation, you really can learn while you earn. You start where you are, with what you have, and live out your dreams one by one by being in the network marketing industry.

I now have more control over my financial destiny, and I have also created some great memories made with my family, my growing "customer community and my brand partners; who are now among my closest friends." For me, there is one dream realized that stands out more than others. The experience was made possible because of me being a "professional" in the network marketing industry.

My mom was a wife and mother of three, and she worked full-time for 30 years as an administrative assistant. To earn extra money, she had a part-time gig typing resumes. My mom was a woman who once took a day off her job to take me to an open audition for the movie "Annie." Even though I didn't get a callback, she was proud of me for applying. She was the one who had the forward thought to take me to hear Les Brown when I was a troubled teen. My mom was my biggest fan. I once asked her what something that she wanted to do was. She said, "I want to do an Alaskan Cruise." As a leader in my network marketing company, I was able to go on the 25th-anniversary company chartered cruise to Alaska, and guess who my guest for this trip of a lifetime was? Yes, my mom. The industry is not perfect, but it works. You can have your dreams. It starts with a "yes."

Contact the Author: Stephanie Y. Oden
Email:questions@stephanieoden.com
Website: www.stephanieoden.com

Saying Yes Brings True Success

By Teresa Selby Fink

Living paycheck to paycheck while growing up gave me no desire to live that way when my husband and I were married in 1993; nonetheless, the pattern continued. From 2000-2009, when our four children were young, my husband, Jerry, was our family's sole breadwinner and our money always felt stretched thin. Each month, he wondered aloud where our money disappeared to as he determined which medical bills to pay after all other bills were met first. Each time he asked, I took his words to mean, "You are terrible at managing the household."

Twice I attempted to contribute to our household funds. I sold beauty and health products with a long-standing and well-known company for a year but stopped when our eldest child was born. Then, I was in a party-planning business for two years but got out when our third child was born. In both companies, I spent far more money on products than I earned, and when I quit each one, I felt as much a failure in managing a business as I did in managing our home.

Aligned with his passion, my husband started a small engine repair business to help make ends meet. His business often kept him home during family outings, and I was often irritated with him for staying home because I felt guilty. I wanted him present in our children's lives, but I knew that my lack of income minimized that opportunity for him. The children were disappointed at his absence from our activities, but as they got older, they expected it. I finally joined the workforce part-time in 2009 to help ease the financial burden. I am still working for the same company today because our debt grew as each child aged and entered the public university system.

Clinical depression and many other health challenges compounded my feelings of failure during my stay-at-home-mom years. In 2016, my mental and physical health was so poor that my husband said he was worried I would not be around to see our children (who now ranged in age from 15-22) get married and have children of their own. Fortunately, a church friend posted on social media about natural health supplements she had fallen in love with and asked to share some information with me. I looked at the information but was skeptical and did not try the products for five months. A looming health screening that threatened to reaffirm a pre-diabetes diagnosis for the fourth straight year persuaded me to give them a try. I had tried multiple times to overcome my sugar addiction but had been unsuccessful. Feeling I had nothing to lose thanks to the 60-day money-back guarantee, I decided to place an order.

While walking me through the ordering process, my friend offered me a wholesale membership with a business opportunity attached just in case I fell in love with the products too. While Jerry was very skeptical that I could make any business successful in our town, he gave me the blessing to sign up as she suggested. He did ask me to wait for three months before I started working the business, but within three weeks, I was sold on the products and wanted to get my business going. Within the first six months, I advanced to the first rank in my company. As of this writing, I am at the same rank.

God answered my prayers for a way to earn money from home, but when He provides an answer, He does not necessarily take away all your problems. Low self-confidence and a negative mindset typically accompany depression, and I was no exception. While my physical and mental health was undergoing positive changes thanks to my products, I still needed a serious mindset shift to see the success I was dreaming about. I found that shift through personal growth and investing in myself. I joined paid business communities starting in June 2018 and began purchasing training courses offered by industry leaders.

In June 2019, I purchased a video training program from a popular network marketing team and started recording daily Facebook Live videos. I continued with the videos but struggled to see their value until I attended a three-day business summit in October 2019. There, I was told of their value by numerous fellow entrepreneurs. Their responses elevated my confidence, and the videos continued as part of my daily operations.

In 2020, I was blessed to meet and work with my lifestyle coach and co-author, Kim Ward. With her help, I worked through numerous personal and business obstacles, and my confidence rose again. Kim introduced me to new business mentors in the summer of 2020, including co-author Stacey Hall, who has had great success building multiple businesses by going for yes rather than no. I can see now that my investments in coaching, various training courses, and multiple business communities with strong mentors are paying off because my business is gaining momentum.

My story is a perfect example of the power of yes. By saying yes to network marketing, I have gained so much. I have better physical and mental health than ever before. I have a tribe of friends—both inside and outside of my company—that support and encourage me in ways that I have never before experienced. I have seen one of my children get married in 2020 and will see another marry in November 2021. I will be present in the life of our first grandchild, who is due to arrive before this book is printed and look forward to the birth of future grandchildren. I will have realized my dream of becoming a book author with this book's release, plus a children's picture book later this year. The money and fulfilled dreams will continue to increase as I grow my business, but as I now know, that success is about so much more than that. True success lies in realizing our potential and positively impacting the lives of others.

I am manifesting my dreams of success. Are you ready to manifest yours?

Contact the Author: Teresa Selby Fink
Email: teresa.s.fink@gmail.com
Visit: www.go.teresafink.com

FROM DARKNESS TO LIGHT

Terry D. Allen

My life before network marketing was filled with grief over the sudden loss of my younger sister. I was tired, and my inner child was curled up in a closet, in total darkness with the door shut tight and no hope of seeing the light. It was exhausting. I was lost even with counseling and the support of my husband and my friends.

Go into direct sales or network marketing no way! I had been asked to do direct sales before and always found a way to say no. However, while at a Home and Garden Show, a friend pushed me toward a vendor demonstrating lipstick. I didn't even wear lipstick. My friend exclaimed, "You need to sell this!" I thought that she was nuts. However, my friend is a force, and honestly, there was no use in arguing with her; I knew I'd lose.

Interestingly, when the first person we asked about signing up as a distributor turned me down, I secretly said, "thank goodness."

"Not so fast," said one of the other distributors. She wrapped me in a warm hug and smiled broadly at me. Her actions touched mt heart and somehow pushed on that closet door. We exchanged contact information, and to my utter surprise, she reached out to me a few days later. We talked for quite some time, and she invited me to her next event out of town the next weekend. I talked with my husband, and he was all for it and full of encouraging support.

So, now committed to an event 2.5 hours from my home, I suddenly remembered that I don't drive! Did I mention that I have panic attacks when driving anywhere—even in my hometown? Even with that epiphany, I knew that this was exactly where I was supposed to be in my soul.

I packed my car, updated my GPS, and had my first real conversation with God in over two years. I told God, "You and you alone are in control; I humbly give this moment and adventure over to you." As I was driving to Corpus Christi, Texas, I waited for the panic attack to appear, but it never came! I arrived and sat in my car crying tears of joy for 30 minutes. I then realized that I drove alone and was spending the weekend with a stranger! Oh, did the realization of that make me laugh! My new upline met me outside with a big bear hug, and the instant calm of knowing "this is where I'm supposed to be" comforted me. The closet door cracked open a little further, and suddenly, there was the tiniest sliver of light! I still had a long way to go, but I now had hope that I would find my way back and out of that dark, lonely closet.

Two years later, I can confidently say my life is even more impressive than I would have ever dreamed. I now confidently and eagerly manage my corporate job, my network marketing career, and multiple teams. I embrace change and address my fears with confidence. I know there are like-minded women to lift me up, cheer me on, and yes, occasionally dust me off. My greatest joy is knowing that I can help empower other women, lift them, encourage them and, yes, dust them off too.

I measure my success by knowing I can change the course of my future and that I could confidently start over! I know that without a doubt, I could earn a living doing anything because I've learned that the real brand, I'm selling is me. I also find it quite remarkable that the knowledge and skills I've developed through network marketing do not sit (quietly) contained in my network marketing career. Those skills spill over into every aspect of my life!

I get a kick when friends, family, and colleagues ask me what I'm doing that's different. I smile and say being an entrepreneur has been the catalyst for my transformation. I am humbly grateful for the opportunities network marketing has brought me. I now travel through my life knowing my inner child is happy, confident, and dancing on a beach while embracing the light—no dark, dreary closets for me.

Contact the Author: Terry Allen
Email: celestialbeautybyTerry@gmail.com

DON'T FIRE YOUR UPLINE

By: Tonia Smith

Never say never.

I had sworn off any type of network marketing due to growing up around it when my parents were in Amway. Nothing in that world appealed to me.

Then about 6 years ago, I was introduced to a product that was life-changing for me, and happened to be a business opportunity, as well. I resisted as long as I could, but finally took the bit and jumped all in.

It wasn't long before I was teaching about the product at the local community college, travelling all over the country to vendor fairs and coaching and supporting my teammates. I was rank advancing, walking stages to receive awards and loving every minute of it.

Then it became like a constant uphill battle and team members would come and go. It became harder and harder to keep my rank and the idea of advancing further just seemed impossible.

My upward trajectory came to a stand-still. So, I left that company and jumped to another "shiny object" ~ thinking a new company was the answer to my prayers. I shot through the ranks and was making money and then hit a brick wall. I started to see the same pattern I experienced before. I was working long hours, sacrificing time with my family and was no longer having fun.

I began to wonder, was network marketing for me? At this point, I wasn't sure, but I knew I had to do something different. I tried reaching out to my upline for answers, but they didn't seem to have the time for me that I felt I needed. I wanted to succeed and make it to the top ~ that was my dream, my vision, my why. I was hurt and angry and blamed my upline for their lack of support.

Then I realized, this was my business and I needed to take charge of it. So, it was up to me to grow and develop my skills as a leader and as a marketer. I discovered the wonderful world of attraction marketing and realized that with these skills, I didn't need an upline to hold my hand.

I learned that it's all about consistency and taking action each and every day that will actually propel you forward. With this new mindset and strategy, I've also learned to enjoy the process. There will be ups and downs, but as long as you keep taking meaningful actions, you'll reach your goals. And in the meantime, you might as well enjoy the journey and appreciate each and every success – no matter how small.

Personally, my driving force has been two-fold – a combination of sheer determination and an eye towards the future. The will to succeed and make network marketing work for me motivated me to push through during the tougher times. That determination propelled me to learn, grow and develop. With that, I held onto the vision I had for my future.

I want to stay active – both mentally and physically – for many years to come. I plan on riding horses until I'm 95. In order to achieve this, I needed something that would keep my mind, body and bank account strong. Network marketing provides this. It keeps me mentally agile, allows me the financial freedom required and provides me the flexibility to maintain an active lifestyle.

Even before I understood the steps, I needed to take to efficiently grow my business, these goals – and my overwhelming desire to accomplish them – helped me to persevere when things weren't going my way.

When I look at where I was versus where I am now, I realize my dream life was never about money. I may not have known it at the time, but my dream life sprang from the growth and development

I acquired through network marketing. And it's because of those lessons that I can now enjoy each moment, relish the journey and consistently build upon the foundation I've laid in order to continue creating the life I desire.

Contact the Author: Tonia Smith
Email: toniaheartstrong@gmail.com
Visit www.toniasmith.com/Hub

WHY ARE YOU (STILL) HITTING YOURSELF?

By Tony Schmaltz

There I was, my wife was glaring at me with unnerving fear as I sat at my desk finishing our bills and budget. I let out a big sigh as I sat back in my chair, dripping with anxiety, realizing we were going to run out of money before we ran out of month. The sinking feeling set in when I realized there wasn't enough money to cover our obligations for the rest of the month. I felt the excruciating pain (of the incurable stress) that goes through your head when you remember you talked your wife into financing a boat, and now you don't know how to pay for it or clothes for the kids. As I sat there, the soul-eating virus consumed me from the inside out as I considered giving up on everyone and everything. I was at a loss for what to do to make sure my wife and kids would have the life I had promised them.

I walked away from the desk and sat on the couch to watch the game, hoping to drown out the bad thoughts about our bills still going through my head. As I sat down on the couch, I felt pressure on my chest like someone was laying brick upon brick on my lungs, making it harder and harder to breathe. Just then, my eight-year-old looked at me with those innocent eyes filled with concern and said, "What's the matter, Daddy?" As I choked back the tears and collected myself, I lied and said, "Nothing, son, everything is okay." It was at that moment that I knew I had to do something different, but what?

Do you remember that game that your older brother or sister would torture you with, the one where they would grab your wrists and then hit you in the face with your own hands? Then they would say, "Why are you hitting yourself?" and no matter how much you struggled, you were stuck taking the punishment. This is the feeling that I had, day in and day out, with our financial struggles; I felt like I was hitting myself, over and over and over. We couldn't 't go on this way; something had to change, and it had to change NOW. It wasn't long after that I discovered the world of network marketing.

When I first found network marketing, I was determined to get rich quickly, to get my family everything they ever dreamed of, and quit my job with a bang. You know what I mean—walk into work, tell off everyone that you didn't like, and then walk out with a big, fat, metaphorical mic drop, BOOM! However, when I got more involved with this business, I met the people I now call family. I started getting mentored by industry leaders and I found so much more. For me, it was a match thrown on gasoline, setting ablaze the fire within me that revolved around non-stop personal development.

In the world of network marketing, I was able to tap into the explosive power of personal choice. It is probably the most powerful tool that anyone can grasp in their journey through life, whether in network marketing or not. When you learn the power of choice, you can take all the negativity in your life, drag it kicking and screaming to the front door and throw it out. When you choose to shift your mindset and stop worrying about what others think, there is no stopping you on your journey to success. So many people fail in the world of network marketing because they are afraid of hearing the word "No" when the word "No" is a teaching moment on the way to "Yes."

After learning about the importance of personal choice, my family and I were happy—happier than we had ever been together, even before making a lot of money. We learned to only care about the things that matter, and that is not using words like "No." Exploring yourself, finding who it is that you are, and what you want leads to happiness. When you live your life as the real you, stop people-pleasing, and own the person you are for yourself and your family, happiness is inevitable. So, stop hitting yourself and be the real you to find your happiness. This is what the network marketing industry did for me and many others who discovered the same truth.

Contact the Author: Tony Schmaltz
Email: tony@tonyschmaltz.com
Visit: www.tonyschmaltz.com

Attraction Marketing: The Authentic Way to Reaching Your Potential

By Tracey Cook

My story is my greatest motivation. It's also my go-to example when I speak about a positive mindset and how saying "yes" can change a life. Often, the reason we fail is that, while it may seem like we are invested in something (we're doing or a part of), our minds do not agree with us. We see ourselves underachieving, failing, and falling short because while our bodies may be present, our minds are far away. If your mind and body are aligned, you become unstoppable. All your dreams and aspirations will be at your fingertips you reach heights you never thought possible before.

In 2018, I started in network marketing while fighting many battles with my health. I needed to contribute to my family's income, and the only way to do this was to work from home. I was using a product that I thought was excellent and needed to reach more people. I reached out to the product's distributor and asked her to teach me how to run my network marketing business.

In the beginning, I wasn't teachable. I ignored good advice and did things the way I thought they were meant to be done. Despite this, my team grew quickly, and I advanced in my rank, earning all sorts of rewards and bonuses. However, I was unfair to my downline because I demanded more from them than was necessary. I was also condescending, and I disappointed many people, mostly myself. Even though I was making progress, I learned the hard way that what I was doing was sabotaging my chances of reaching my full potential. I was closing doors that were opened (for my benefit) and opening doors that were not mutually beneficial.

Everything changed in 2018 when I found a group of "professional" network marketers and a mentor who taught attraction marketing. It felt so right. I changed companies, started to learn all over again, and rebuilt myself.

In 2019, I flew from Perth, Western Australia, to Florida for a reality show that I was fortunate to be a part of and one that changed my perspective. I learned the simple pathway to a successful career in network marketing. It involves:

- Showing up
- Impacting people
- Marketing product/services properly
- Connecting the right way
- Doing your business the right way

Attraction marketing felt so authentic to me. It's simply seeing if people are open to looking at your product, service, or opportunity. I found a home amongst a community of empowering, supportive people who were also on their journey (to the top) and who desired progress. From there, I learned never to settle for less than is attainable, and I was more motivated than before. I learned from the mistakes of others, so I didn't need to make more. Before long, I was reaching heights that surprised even me.

Choose to say "yes" today! Work with a positive mindset, and you will create positive interactions, serve the community, and leave a legacy behind that makes the world a much better place than you met it. Through "the power of yes," I have learned marketing strategies that have helped my business methods connect more authentically, grow exponentially, and my family's financial outlook has been changed dramatically.

Today, I am more than just a woman who sells products on the internet; I am a wife, a mother, and a grandmother who has helped and is still helping other individuals (and their families) move closer to their dream lives through consistency, passion, hard work, and authenticity. You can achieve that too. It doesn't matter how long it takes as long as you never give up and deeply believe that you will get to your destination.

Contact the Author: Tracey Cook
Email: contact@traceyleecook.com
Visit www.traceyleecook.com
Follow Tracey Cook on Social Media
Visit www.facebook.com/traceyleecook1

No Holding Back Secrets Anymore

By Xenia Wignan

You know that saying, "What is meant to be, will be?" Well, I respectfully and adamantly disagree! You see I had a secret for most of my life. A secret that I was ashamed to let out. One that I did not tell anyone until 2017. When I finally told my partner, it was such a relief!

Let me take you back a few years. I had a normal childhood, got good grades, went to university and was grateful to find an entry-level corporate job. Over the next several years, I progressed with my employer and found myself in a role of serving others as an employment counsellor.

Although I was happy to have this job, I was restless. I used to joke with people and say, "I still don't know what I want to be when I grow up." I said this up to the age of 43.

I felt like I was just living in a fog, just surviving, and doing what I had to do every day. I felt no passion, no purpose and wondered if this was what life was going to be like. It made me sad to think that this was the case but then I would immediately feel guilty. What I had was more than so many people, and though I should just accept where life took me and not be ungrateful.

So, I kept doing what I was "supposed to do" and went on to get married and have three boys. My boys are my world, and they have changed me forever. I just couldn't stand the thought that living without passion and purpose would also be their destiny.

Unfortunately, I could not think too much about this for the next ten years. I was in the middle of a very toxic and abusive relationship. So much happened during my 10-year marriage including physical, emotional, and financial abuse. I felt worthless. It took everything in me just to get up in the morning, shower, go to work and take care of my children. I was completely numb and didn't have a clue what tomorrow would hold.

As you may have guessed, my marriage ended. I was left with a mountain of debt and not only did I worry about paying the bills, I was also in danger of losing our home.

As we muddled through the next couple of years, I found myself trying to figure out where to go from there. I was still working at a job I had no passion for, still not financially stable, and still feeling like I had no purpose.

The only difference—I could now explore this burning desire that I had buried for so long. I was out of the fog of survival mode and able to slowly heal and think a little clearer. I learned about boundaries, self-worth, and being happy.

I even started to feel a little excitement about my life. So, when I was introduced to an opportunity where I could use amazing products and make some extra money, I was all in! I didn't know much about this type of business, but it provided me with hope. Hope that I could build something of my own. Hope that I could set an example for my boys and start building a little financial security for my family.

I dove in immediately. I made some sales and signed up a team member. Although I was not with my first company long, I saw what I could never "unsee," the hope of creating my dream life. I also learned that this industry is all about self-development. The more I learned about myself and how to be happy, the more I would succeed! The more money I made, the more I could help people.

I have a growing team of amazing women now, and I thank God that I was introduced to network marketing. I will continue to inspire that single mom who doesn't think she has options and help her see that she is unlimited in what she can accomplish to create her own dream life!

I am personally aiming for multiple seven figures because the more money I make, the more I can give. I know for a fact that the last two Christmases and birthdays were a lot less stressful on me because of my business.

Oh, I almost forgot! You know that secret that I mentioned? I had told my love, Miki, that I felt like I was meant for more. When I found network marketing, I found my more.

Contact the Author: Xenia Wignan
Email: Wignanx@gmail.com
www.facebook.com/xenia.wignan

EPILOGUE

By Stacey Hall

I have had the goal to produce this book for many years.

Having written two #1 best-selling books previously, it was important to me to make it possible for others to express their voice, make a difference and leave a legacy that will love on long after they are gone.

With this Power of YES book series, I feel I have achieved my goal in a soul-satisfying way.

Throughout my career, as successful as it is, there were many times I would have picked up a book like this to receive encouragement and a reminder to keep my eye on what is truly important…especially on those days that were less-than-wonderful.

Each of the Authors you have met in this book are people I respect deeply for how they generously serve so many people through their business.

And, in addition to these Authors, I have many more people to acknowledge for their support and encouragement in bringing this book series into reality.

First and foremost, I acknowledge and appreciate the support and constant guidance I receive from God, the Divine Creator, the Gracious, the Powerful, the Generous, the Loving!

Next, my appreciation and loves goes to my husband, Bill, who has been my Partner in every way that I could ever want a Partner to be.

My respect and admiration to Lil Barcaski and her team at GWN Publishing for also being just as committed to publishing and distributing this beautiful and enlightening book as I am!

My ever-lasting gratitude goes out to the founders, staff, coaches and members of My Lead System Pro. There are thousands associated with this organization that deserve to be mentioned by name. And because of space constrictions, thanks for understanding that I am specifically mentioning Brian Fanale, Todd Schlomer, Norbert Orlewicz, James Fanale, Melanie Lozano, Rhonda Reiter, Troy Boyd, JP Letnick, Jimmy Ybarra, Anthony Jackson and Joe Tarin, who made it possible for me to know all the others!!

The endorsements for this book make my heart smile each time I read them. Thank you to (in alphabetical order) Erin Birch, Haylee Crowley, Mark Harbert, Elsa Morgan, Jim Packard, Jackie Sharpe, Antonio Thompson, and Dr. Joe Vitale.

My appreciation extends to and surrounds everyone I have ever attracted into my life – my family, friends, clients, coaches, teachers, publishers of my previous books, my upline sponsors, my team members, business and cross-line brainstorming partners, those who help me care for my health and well-being, and the network marketing companies, whose products I and the Authors in this book have been blessed to represent.

Special recognition goes out to my pups – Lucy and Francesca (known as 'Frankie) for all the walks we missed and the reduction in cuddle time while I was producing this book. I am putting on my walking shoes now and getting your leashes. Let's go.

My appreciation extends to each reader of these words.

To learn more about the "Go For YES" sales success formula mentioned throughout this book, reach out to the Authors or visit book.goforyeschallenge.com.

You will discover:

A 4-step plan to authentically sell more of your products in a way that makes you (and them) feel amazing.

How to identify your audience's pain points so you can speak to their soul and influence them to take action.

The source for never-ending content ideas and daily strategy for what to post and when for maximum results.

Where to establish your social media presence to connect with your audience who are ready to buy.

And you will find satisfaction and a successful way to make more sales and serve more people.

I would love to hear from you.

Send your endorsements, comments and questions to me at stacey@staceyhallonline.com

———————

"When I think of genuine heartfelt leadership I think of Stacey Hall. She is an incredible trainer in the profession of Network Marketing. She has a proven track record helping people get results using her "Go For YES" formula.

Devour every bit of wisdom she has gathered here. You will NOT be disappointed!"

– Mark Harbert
Marketing Expert & Trainer
MarkHarbert.com

AUTHOR INDEX

BUSINESS STRATEGY & DEVELOPMENT

Once we find the pain points, hone the messaging, and get clarity for you and your business, our team brings the goods!

LONGBARCREATIVES.COM | 727-348-6682

GHOSTWRITERSNETWORK.COM

Ghostwriting
Editing
Coaching
Publishing
Writers Retreats
Book Marketing

GFADDESIGN.COM

Branding | Logos
Graphic Design
Web Design
Printing
Promotional Products
SMM Management

Proudly Published by

A DIVISION OF LONGBAR CREATIVE SOLUTIONS, INC.

GWNPUBLISHING.COM